*For Dan Neal, who made it possible.*

—Candy Moulton

*To my daughter, Kelly Whiteaker,*
*and my son, Kit Kevin Kern.*

—Ben Kern

*This book is based on our true-life experiences*
*traveling along the Oregon Trail,*
*although the names and other details*
*relating to certain individuals have been changed.*
*Out of respect for the four teen-aged girls*
*who shared this trip with us,*
*and at the request of their father,*
*their names are changed.*

# Contents

Ben Kern has worked as ranch hand, cowboy, rodeo contestant and pick-up man, and logger. He was born in Nebraska, but has spent most of his life in Wyoming and Oregon. He is retired from the Casper Parks and Recreation Department, and now works on various Wyoming ranches, assisting with calving, lambing and other outdoor work. Since his 1993 wagon trip over the Oregon Trail, Ben has continued driving wagons during the summer time on various cutoffs of the Oregon Trail. He hopes to follow the Meek Cutoff, the Applegate Trail, and to retrace the route of the Mormon Trail from Nauvoo, Illinois, to Salt Lake City, Utah. He has a daughter, Kelly Whiteaker, a son, Kit Kevin Kern, and three grandchildren. When he's not out on the trail, he makes his home in Casper, Wyoming.

Candy Moulton has worked on her family's ranch, as a soda jerk, and as a newspaper and magazine reporter, photographer and editor. She writes regularly for a number of western publications including the *Casper Star Tribune, American Cowboy*, and *Persimmon Hill.* She is the editor of *Roundup Magazine*, official publication of Western Writers of America, and the author of *Legacy of the Tetons: Homesteading in Jackson Hole* and *Roadside History of Wyoming.* She co-authored *Steamboat: Legendary Bucking Horse* with Flossie Moulton. Forthcoming books include *Roadside History of Nebraska, Salt Lake City Uncovered*, and a history of her hometown, Encampment, Wyoming. She and her husband, Steve, have two children, Shawn and Erin Marie.

FOREWORD

# The Great Medicine Road

MANY CENTURIES AGO, the Cheyenne culture hero Sweet Medicine prophesied that the Whites would come: "Soon you will find among you a people who have hair all over their faces, and whose skin is white.... There will be many of these people," he said, "so many that you cannot stand before them...there will be things moving over dry land in which these people will be."

They called the trail these strange new people followed "The Great Medicine Road of the Whites" and believed it possessed supernatural power. Only today, more than one hundred fifty years later, can we fully grasp the depth of that truth.

By 1850 the overland trails had become pulsing arteries of transportation, leading emigrants to the western territories, miners to the California goldfields, and military troops to posts in the far west. When the traffic finally slowed to a trickle in 1867, over 350,000 people and millions of stock animals had made the journey. Their stories, written in journals, diaries and letters, gave birth to what can rightly be called the "creation myth" of a nation.

The overland emigrant, fleeing economic depression in the east, often lonely and heartsick, has become one of our culture heroes. The other hero that emerged from the overland migrations is the Native American fighting for his way of life. In myth, it is the hero who dares to forsake home and hearth and ventures forth to slay monsters—from the white perspective, the monster was the trail itself. Like a twisting serpent, it threatened to choke the life from them.

The single thread of each story, when woven together with all the others, is *our* story. The story of America.

That is not to say that all Oregon Trail travelers found their journeys heroic.

Harriet Williams, in 1865, wrote, "I felt that the same energy, time and money spent in some other way would be such a benefit to mankind, and who would go to Oregon as long as there was land to live on anywhere else?"

Jennie Wriston said that she had looked in geographies for the "Great American Desert" and found it described as, "an arid waste, inhabited by savages, wild beast, and serpents, and on which no rain ever fell in a reasonable natural manner," and said she believed it. Catherine Haun agreed, writing, "I shudder yet at the thought of the ugliness…."

Emigrant diaries record many mundane details, the weather, the lack of water or wood for fires, the sight of the first Indian, or buffalo. Some found the journey thrilling, but many more suffered agonizing hardships.

Rampant cholera, smallpox, heat, choking dust, fear of drowning while crossing swollen streams, the terror of the first snow storm, the loss of loved ones—all of these things were the many "elephants" of the trail, the monsters that had to be overcome if they were to make it to the golden paradise that awaited them.

And a few found paradise in the journey itself.

"I could not help but wonder at the beauty…" Lavinia Porter wrote in 1860 on her way to Oregon. "Above us was the bright dome of a heaven so free from all earthly smoke and vapor, so clear and transparent, that the stars seemed closer and shone with an exceeding brilliancy. The air was filled with a balmy sweetness, and yet so limpid and clear that even in the starlight we could catch glimpses of the shimmering trees in the distant river."

Elizabeth Cumming wrote, "Never have I imagined any thing like what I have seen. Do not think me affected when I say my heart *ached*. It was *physical* pain produced in me by what I saw.... The most unearthly, weird, wild scenes crowd my memory."

The overland trails posed particular problems for the native peoples. As early as 1842, the Sioux told the United States government that the trails were closed, and to emphasize that declaration they captured two emigrants who had stopped at Independence Rock in Wyoming. Legendary mountain man Thomas Fitzpatrick successfully negotiated for the release of those emigrants, but the Sioux sent a final message: "Any whites which should hereafter be found on it," meaning the trail, "would meet with certain destruction."

The white tide quickly became more than a curiosity to the tribes. By 1843 the loss of game and vegetation was apparent. The emigrants complained that the trains which passed in front of them left the trail desolate. One member of a wagon train hunting party reported that the "great quantity of cattle" the people ahead of him herded, "made the grazing very scarce and bad for us, besides that, the buffalo were hunted all out of our path."

The Indians agreed. In 1845, the Superintendent of Indian Affairs in St. Louis reported that the plains tribes, "who subsist on game, complain that the buffalo are wantonly killed and scared off, which renders their only means of subsistence every year more precarious."

That same year, Colonel Stephen Kearny assembled the

Sioux outside of Fort Laramie, in what was then Dakota Territory, but is now in eastern Wyoming, and told the chiefs that their Great Father in Washington had sent him to visit them. "I am opening a road for your white brethren," he told them, "and your Great Father directs that his red children shall not attempt to close it up."

Thomas Fitzpatrick was appointed Indian Agent for the Upper Platte and Arkansas region on August 6, 1846—a year of critical importance to America. During a feast given by the Indians for the emigrants that year, one Sioux chief lamented, "This country belongs to the red man, but his white brethren travel through, shooting the game and scaring it away. Thus the Indian loses all that he depends upon to support his wives and children. The children of the red man cry for food, but there is no food."

Indian raiding along the trails increased. When Brigham Young led his Mormon pioneers along the trail in 1847, he was stopped by the Pawnees. The Indians demanded payment to let him pass. Young agreed to pay them, but the Pawnees said his payment was too small, and that he must turn around and go back. When Young protested, the Pawnees said that they did not like the whites to pass through their country because they feared all the buffalo would be killed or driven off by the wagons and their hunters.

In 1849, D.D. Mitchell, Superintendent of Indian Affairs, said that the Indians considered the depredations to be "just retaliation for the destruction of their buffalo, timber and grass, etc., caused by the vast numbers of whites passing through their country without their consent."

But if the Indians were suffering from the impacts of the trail, so were the emigrants.

In 1850 both cholera and smallpox ravaged the trains.

White victims from cholera alone numbered approximately 2,500, while the Shoshone tribe lost fifty percent of its population to the disease. Emigrant Albert Sortore noted the multitude of fresh graves along the trail with horror, saying his train was, "scarcely out of sight of grave diggers." California bound Carlisle Abbott said that cholera struck "like a cyclone on both sides of the Platte."

Between St. Joseph, Missouri, and Fort Laramie, Dakota Territory, emigrants passed a fresh grave an average of once every quarter mile that year.

At the 1851 Fort Laramie Treaty session, Superintendent D.D. Mitchell opened the meeting by saying that the Great Father in Washington knew of the tribes' suffering and that "any injuries they might have sustained in consequence of the destruction of their game, timber and grass, by the passage of whites through their country, would be fairly paid for by the government of the United States." In exchange, the Great Father asked that the tribes grant his white children safe passage through Indian territories. The tribes said they would, signed the document, and Mitchell wrote that "nothing but bad management" could ever break the treaty.

But bad management was the hallmark of government involvement. Before the tribes had even returned to their winter camps, Congress had altered the terms of the agreement, cutting length of payment from the agreed upon fifty years, to ten years. The impact was stunning and would lead to the Plains Indian Wars.

The Sioux, Fitzpatrick wrote in 1853, are in "abject want of food half the year, and their reliance for that scanty supply, in the rapid decrease of the buffalo, is fast disappearing.... Their women are pinched with want and their children constantly crying out with hunger." The tribes, he wrote were in a "starving state."

The emigrants weren't having an easy time of it, either. Between 1852 and 1853 approximately 70,000 people crossed the trail. The sheer numbers decimated the land and polluted the water sources. Richard Hickan wrote, "We done some good traveling, for we were in the midst of sickness, pain and death, and thought if we could manage to out travel the bulk of immigration we would not be so much exposed to the cholera, measles and smallpox, which is scattered along the road." Ezra Meeker said that the trail looked like a battlefield. "The dead lay sometimes in rows of fifties or more...crowds of people were continually hurrying past us in their desperate haste to escape...."

When Thomas Fitzpatrick, diplomat and defender of the tribes, died in February of 1854, the situation grew critical. Subsequent agents altered the methods of distributing the annuities. Rather than taking the goods into the Indian camps, they required each tribe to come to a central location to pick them up. Often the goods did not arrive until after winter had set in and several feet of snow covered the ground. Under such conditions, the tribes could not travel to retrieve their food, so few received the goods that were due them.

That summer, as instructed, the Sioux came to the fort to await their promised annuities. They waited peacefully for two months with no word as to when the goods might arrive. Hungry, destitute without the government's payments, they found a lame cow wandering alone near the Oregon Trail, killed, and ate it.

On August 18, the Mormon owners of the cow reported to officers at Fort Laramie that the Indians had stolen the cow. A detachment of troops was sent to apprehend the "thief." Lieutenant John Grattan, barely a year out of West Point, commanded the detachment. Grattan demanded that the band turn over the culprit. The Sioux tried to explain that they had not known the cow belonged to anyone, since its owners were nowhere in sight, but Chief Conquering Bear said that if the soldiers would wait until the agent arrived with their annuities, they would gladly pay the owners for the loss. Grattan refused, demanded that the thief be turned over, and readied his men. When Conquering Bear hesitated, the brash young lieutenant ordered his men to fire. The chief was killed. Grattan's major artillery pieces, however, were set too high and his volley flew over the heads of the Sioux. The warriors decimated Grattan's command, then rode to the nearby trading houses of Pierre Choteau and Company. Screaming that their children were starving, the Sioux ordered the keeper, Bordeaux, to turn over all the goods he had, and rode off.

Indian depredations became so frequent that terrified white travelers complained to Washington. In reply, one Arapaho chief said that his people were ill from smallpox and unable to hunt; without raiding the trails, he said, his people would have starved.

The only solution, as the tribes saw it, was to stop the travel on the roads.

In 1857 a pack train of army topographical engineers left Fort Laramie to conduct a reconnaissance of the Black Hills. Lieutenant Warren Kemble was in command. His crew was stopped by a Sioux war party in September. In a torrential rain storm, Chief Black Shield told Kemble: "The Great Father asked us for a road along the Platte, and we gave it to him. We gave him one along the White River and another along the Missouri.... This is the last place left to us, and if we give it up we must die. We had better die fighting like men."

The bloody Indian Wars which plagued the nation for the next two decades ended with the tribes being confined to reservations, and white civilization spreading across the continent.

I have chronicled the above for a reason, and not just to provide historical context for what you are about to read.

In *Wagon Wheels* you will journey with modern trail travelers and hear them describe their own "elephants," and I want you to think of something as you do: America in 1996 is torn by cultural warfare. People in the West, families who have lived on the land for generations, are watching their ways of life vanish to the onslaught of a different value system, a different understanding of what makes life meaningful. The modern trail travelers you are about to join are going to tell you, better than any politician, historian or sociologist ever can, what it means to be a Westerner—what it means to depend upon and cherish the land.

Each entry in *Wagon Wheels* is a moment of profound examination of the world, an attempt to bring life into sharper focus than we usually see it. Candy, Ben, and Earl manage a feat of near magic. They extend their hands, reach across the gulf that separates them from their readers, and draw them into a stunning new world of magnificent animals, violent weather, and friendships forged of suffering. These pages are also filled with crystal clear observations of the dramatic changes the land was undergoing in 1993.

Perhaps I should have said they draw us into a very old world, one where Majesty and its destruction still haunt the heart.

I read this book very carefully, knowing I was reading not just for me, but for all the dreamers in the history of this country who would have given their very lives to feel the freedom that Candy, Ben and Earl describe. It is a great national tragedy that many people in modern America cannot even imagine a place where a man or woman can stand and gaze into infinity, without fences, telephone poles, or houses to mar the view. Or imagine why it matters.

A century from now historians will be poring over this book, trying to glean every detail, comparing descriptions of wildlife, marveling at the stories of wild horse herds roaming the plains, documenting the distinct western language used, studying the variations in gender roles along the trail and comparing them to roles played by the original trail travelers.

*Wagon Wheels* is an extraordinary resource, but not just for scholars. All people who cherish the shreds of frontier that still exist in America, and the values that arise from them, will clutch this book to their hearts. If nothing else, readers will see that the western experience is, and always has been, a thing of the land, that hardship is the price of freedom, and its exceedingly great reward.

But Candy, Ben and Earl can tell you about these things much better than I can.

Enjoy.

— Kathleen O'Neal Gear
former Wyoming State Historian,
author of *Thin Moon and Cold Mist,*
and co-author, with W. Michael Gear,
of *People of the Silence.*

# Acknowledgements

During the period from 1992 to 1994 as Ben Kern and I traveled across the Oregon Trail route by automobile and in a replica Conestoga wagon pulled by horses and mules, we kept journals of our experiences. This book is a combination of those writings, the historic writings of travelers who preceded us, and interviews and research associated with the settlement of the American West.

The seed was planted for this book as we first traveled in Nebraska, and it grew on our trip across Wyoming as we became travel partners and friends. Its real push to fruition came in a bar in Riverton, Wyoming, when former Bureau of Land Management and Wyoming State Historian Kathy Gear and I had a Coke together.

"You simply must write the story," Kathy told me. "It is a picture of life on the trail as it is today, at this moment. It will be as valuable to researchers and historians in one hundred years as the journals and diaries of people who crossed the trail 150 years ago are now."

Ben and I completed our trip and journals, and we talked about putting it all together. It took us quite a while to collect our thoughts and get them on paper and took us longer to see it published. We are indeed fortunate that Earl Leggett, who traveled with us on the Oregon Trail, agreed to add his perspective.

Besides spurring us to write the book, Kathy Gear provided valuable research materials, which made our job so much easier, and gave me a twenty dollar bill as insurance when I was down to my last dollar and two hundred miles from home. She is a special kind of friend. Even further, she agreed to write the foreword to this book, when she had deadlines to meet for her own novels about the American West.

Other people helped us in our search for information and understanding of the trail. Those who served a primary role included Chuck Coon, Wyoming Division of Tourism; Mary Ethel Emanuel, Nebraska Tourism; Dan Neal and Wyoma Groenenberg of the Casper Star-Tribune; the staff at the Wyoming State Museum and Archives, particularly Ann Nelson, Jean Brainard, Roger Joyce, LaVaughn Breshnahan, and Paula West Chavoya; and Rick Ewig at the American Heritage Center, University of Wyoming. For letting us quote from their work, we appreciate Deirdre Stoelzle and Claudette Ortiz. For putting up with my absences, I thank my family, Steve, Shawn, and Erin Marie.

We are grateful for advice and assistance from Gregory Franzwa, Susan Butruille, and Randy Wagner. Many people whom we met along the trail play a part in this story, and we are glad to have met them. In many cases we now call them friends. They include Connie Chamberlain, Eric Burke, Whitey Bowhay, Buck Case, Dave Bowhay, Les and Ruth Broadie, Skinner Collins, Edna and Morris Carter Sr., Dan and Juleen Naffsinger, Leslie Marchando, Donny Marincic, Ray Tinker, Joe Vogel, Stan Vogel, Bobby Lee, and many, many other people who visited with us and traveled the ruts of the Oregon Trail. We particularly want to remember the late Phil Marincic, a fine hand on the trail and a good man to cross the river with. We appreciate the sacrifice and pioneer spirit of the family which traveled the route with us, but at their request we have not focused on their leadership or participation in this trip and we have not used their real names.

Finally we value the role Nancy Curtis plays in this story. She is our editor and publisher and brings our story to you from the high plains of Wyoming. She has a kinship with the trail, like we do, because it crosses her family's ranch.

This book is our story of the trail. It is about the people we met, the towns we visited, and most of all the land we saw.

— CANDY MOULTON
AND BEN KERN

INTRODUCTION

# The Journey: Climb Aboard

*What an absolute test of physical endurance, patience, common sense and survival.*
MARY CRAWFORD, FARM EDITOR
SCOTTSBLUFF (NEBRASKA) STAR HERALD, JUNE 26, 1993

FRESH FACES TURNED westward a century and a half ago as the greatest pioneer movement in American history got underway. At the beginning only a dim trace across the land marked the Oregon Trail. Indians and mountain men had used the route for years. In the 1840s Americans started an exodus to the West. From 1843 to 1873 some 350,000 people traveled the trail turning it from faint tracks to a clear road often scarred by deep ruts cut through the sod and soil and rock.

The story of the western migration is one of both triumph and tragedy. Those who made the trip on the Oregon, California, and Mormon Trails faced great obstacles. Many died along the way and are buried in unmarked graves.

Long before Oregon Fever, trappers and traders beat a path up the rivers and over the prairie grass as they sought fur in the West. The employees of the Rocky Mountain Fur Company, American Fur Company, Hudson Bay Company, and Northwest Fur Company tramped over the West. The earliest French trappers sought pelts in the late 1700s. By 1810 British workers set their lures, and the Americans launched their full-scale efforts to gain control of the beaver market after 1823. The earliest trappers relied on a system of fixed-location forts to sell or trade their plunder for supplies. But the fur industry changed in 1825 when General William H. Ashley launched the first mountain rendezvous on the Henrys Fork of the Green River. However, beaver went out of style and prices plummeted by 1840. The rendezvous system petered out by 1843 when a final gathering took place.

Astorians led by Robert Stuart heading from Fort Astoria, Oregon, in 1812 crossed the Rocky Mountains at the pass south of the Yellowstone River headwaters. They noted the gentle incline and decline of the mountains and, though Stuart wasn't entirely certain exactly where his party was, he knew the pass would allow for future crossings.

In 1824, William Sublette "re-discovered" South Pass, a natural crossing area used for generations by Native Americans, and eight years later Lieutenant Benjamin L. E. Bonneville took the first wagons over the pass. In 1835, missionaries Marcus Whitman and Samuel Parker and their wives crossed to Oregon to deliver their Christian message to the Indians.

The West's legendary mountain men Jedediah Smith, William and Milton Sublette, Joe Meek, Jim Bridger, Jim Beckwourth, Hugh Glass, and David Jackson trapped the western streams, explored the mountains, and reveled in the wild lifestyle. In 1842 the old mountain men—many of whom were only in their forties—saw the first canvas-topped wagons roll across the prairie ripping the fragile grasses and the salt sage from the alkali soil. Some of the trappers served as guides. Others watched a way of life dissolve into the dust.

By 1843, some mountain men had gone under, others had

gone back to towns and cities east of the Mississippi, and the rest had realized life is an ever-changing proposition. They guided John Charles Frémont as he mapped the West and took credit for the discoveries they showed him—places they'd earlier learned of from Indians of the region.

Jim Bridger grabbed an opportunity by building a trading post at the far side of present-day Wyoming. Located on the back side of South Pass, Fort Bridger signaled Bridger's emergence from mountain man to entrepreneur.

From 1843 when Oregon Trail travel officially started until 1873 when the western trail traffic generally ceased because it was easier to ride the new transcontinental railroad, more than 350,000 people crossed the prairies of Missouri, Kansas, and Nebraska, and the mountains of Wyoming, Idaho, and Oregon.

The travelers didn't follow a single highway west, instead they followed a corridor that served the Oregon, California, and Mormon Trails, and that also became the route of the Pony Express and Creighton transcontinental telegraph.

Their stories are remarkable. The travelers were young and old. Their trek hazardous. The commonly-held notion that the biggest danger on the trails was hostile Indians is one myth of the West. More people died from accidents and disease than Indian attack.

In 1993, Americans marked the sesquicentennial of the Oregon Trail. Communities along the trail celebrated; but for the Native Americans the trek in 1843 and the anniversary in 1993 gave no cause for celebration. The Oregon Trail changed their way of life forever as travelers polluted streams, desiccated the range, displaced wildlife, and brought disease.

The tribes had several names for the trail. The Shoshone under Chief Washakie helped the travelers, but they called the trail the River of Destruction. The Sioux referred to it as

"Wasicu Canku: White Man Road." After they signed the 1851 treaty, the Sioux began to call it the "Holy Road" partially, perhaps, because the emigrants and the military acted as though they had a God-given right to cross the land. Further, the tribes thought the trail held a certain power—a spirituality tied to the land itself—a concept that evolved from plains people's belief that the land itself was a living thing possessing a soul. They didn't believe anyone could own the land, however, they did subscribe to the notion that the trails had great "medicine," thus the term "Holy Road."

As in the earlier migration, thousands of people followed the route in 1993. They rode in cars and buses, they rode bicycles and walked along the pathway. Only a handful crossed all or part of the trail using wagons for transportation. In the spirit of the pioneers, Ben Kern hitched a team in Missouri and drove a Conestoga wagon out of Independence on May 2, 1993, to cross the plains, prairie, and mountains.

Ben headed west with his uncle Buck Case of Lewistown, Montana. They traveled with another Wyoming family, here called Shawn Reed and his daughters Erin, Marie, Leeann, and Kris. Down the trail a bit, a mule-drawn wagon from Oregon, driven by Earl Leggett of Aurora, joined them. I traveled with them in Nebraska, Wyoming, Idaho, and Oregon.

Along the way we met a diverse group of people and saw what a century and a half can do to the land.

It's time to climb aboard the wagon, take your seat, and travel the ruts of the Oregon Trail corridor, seeing it through the eyes of the emigrants who made the trek in 1843 or 1850 or some other early year and the more modern viewpoint of Ben Kern, myself, Earl Leggett, and other participants on the 1993 sesquicentennial wagon train.

As Ben would say, "We're gonna go now…."

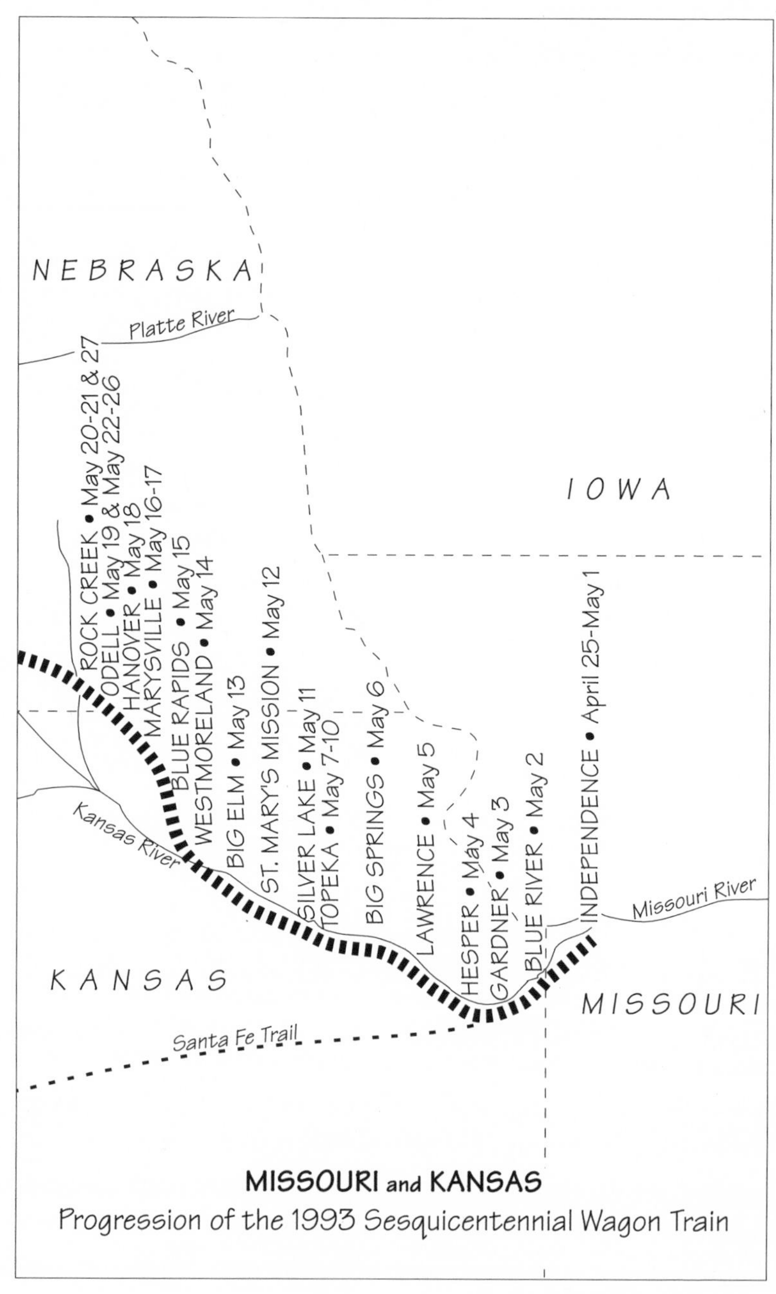


**MISSOURI and KANSAS**
Progression of the 1993 Sesquicentennial Wagon Train

PART ONE:

# *Missouri & Kansas*

*Finally the sun shined and it did not even rain.*
—Ben Kern, May 16, 1993

A light salt and pepper stubble covered Ben Kern's face in mid-April 1993, as he set off on the adventure of his lifetime. Wearing new indigo-colored jeans and an older and slightly-out-of-shape black Stetson, Ben threw the last of his gear into his brown Chevy pickup. With a quick nod to himself, he climbed behind the wheel to begin an odyssey. Since his father had taught him how to drive a team while harvesting hay in eastern Wyoming half a century earlier, Ben had dreamed of crossing America's emigrant trails in a covered wagon.

His chance had finally come. He would travel the ruts of the Oregon Trail in a wagon. Ben's trek started at his home in Evansville, Wyoming, just a stone's throw from one historic Oregon Trail bridge.

Ben Kern:

BK April 15, 1993. My Uncle Buck Case and I left Evansville, Wyoming, for Mitchell, South Dakota, with two wagons on my trailer behind my Chevy pickup. We're going to Doug Hansen's Wheel and Wagon Shop to pick up four sets of running gears. We'll stay in Hot Springs, South Dakota, tonight.

BK April 16. We got to Hansen's shop about noon, loaded the running gears, and headed for Gardner, Kansas, to a farm where the horses and mules we will use on our trip across the Oregon Trail are on pasture.

BK April 17. We drove all day and all night and got in about 4:00 A.M. I laid down for awhile and then went to work unloading the wagons. Buck and I gathered the horses out of the pasture and put them in the corrals on hay and grain rations. It is real pretty and green here. The grass is about six inches high.

BK April 18–24. We started putting things together. Buck and I are camping. We put the running gears together. I stained them with linseed oil and oak stain, three coats. Our new harness and collars had been shipped to the farm. We started putting harness together and fitting collars. Each set of harness and each collar needs to be custom fitted to the horses to make their job easier and prevent irritation as they pull the wagons to Oregon.

We are working the horses on a sled. We use a sled because the horses are up and agoing and want to run away if they can. The sled is big with a large box and heavy. It is a good workout for the horses. We hitch up and drive all the teams several times a day. I am working Tom and Jerry, the mules. When purchased they had worked fine at the sale, but now they are wild, hard to get along with, and need a lot of work. I've been working them every day, several hours a day.

We have a lot of rain and thunderstorms. It rains every day and knocked the power out a couple of times. The lightning hit a big tree right by the house, it was a severe storm. It's April 20 and we have things pretty well put together. Our cook came from Omaha and is cooking for Buck and I.

Buck and I are having fun working the horses every day, we

*Buck Case, left, and Ben Kern, holding Tom the mule.* (Ben Kern Photo)

did have a couple of good run aways. When I first drove the Percheron team, Mark and Mike, with the big wagon, the noise that the big wagon created scared them and we had a good run away. I circled around the ranch house a couple of times and finally in the field got them stopped.

Around April 23 the rest of the wagons arrived and we finished putting them together. We still don't have the canvas tops for the new wagons.

BK April 25. We loaded the horses and wagons and came to Independence, Missouri, to Frontier Park, and made camp. We picketed the horses just east of Frontier Museum and set up our camp on the lawn by the museum. The place where we have our horses staked out is called the "Breaking Ground." This is where people in the 1840s left to go on the Oregon Trail. At that time there was a lot of trading stock for sale and many of the animals were wild, as we have experienced with the horses and mules we bought. The area provided a place for the pioneers to work new stock, just as we had done, before they were hitched up for the trail. There was also a big spring, where the pioneers could fill their water barrels.

THOSE WHO FOLLOWED the Oregon Trail started from many points on the Missouri River, but historians agree the true beginning of the trail is in Independence, Missouri, at the southwest corner of Courthouse Square.

Like a braid, from Courthouse Square one branch went south, down Liberty Street and along the Blue Ridge following the trace marked by Santa Fe traders. A different route went west on Lexington Street headed generally toward Westport, which is now in Kansas City, Missouri.

On April 22, 1849, James A. Pritchard wrote:

JP 1849. Indipendence is a handsome flourishing town with a high situation, three miles from the Missouri River on the South side And Surrounded by one of the most beautiful & fertile countries of any Town in the Nation…Emegrants were encamped in every direction for miles around the place awaiting the time to come for their departure. Such were the crowded condition of the Streets of [Independence] by long trains of Ox teams mule teams men there with stock for Sale and men there to purchase stock that it was all most impossible to pass along.

BEN KERN:

BK April 26–May 1. We've had a couple of days that the

weather was pretty good and the sun shined a little bit. We hooked our horses to the wagons and drove the streets of Independence hauling people hoping to get the horses used to the traffic and people. The horses are really fat and shiny and hard to handle. I left Tom and Jerry back at the farm as they are not ready for the traffic. Tom and Jerry are red roan Belgian cross mules and are a pretty team. We got our canvas tops for our new wagons.

BK May 2. The day Buck and I have been looking forward to! It is pouring down rain, but it is still a very special day. The Museum directors gave us a big celebration and the mayor of Independence gave us a proclamation. We packed all the mail that we will carry to Oregon—including a letter from the Mayor of Independence, Missouri, to the Mayor of Independence, Oregon,—about one thousand other pieces from all over the world. There are a lot of TV and news reporters. As we left the museum they played the song "Oregon Bound."

This indeed is a very special moment as we head to the wagons and prepare to leave. My team is Mark and Mike. Marie drives the number two wagon and her team is Jim and Prince, Leeann drives the number three wagon and her team is Maggie and Molly, Kris drives the number four wagon and her team is Jack and Mowitz. Erin drives the fifth wagon and her team is Towsky and Jumbo. Shawn Reed is the trail captain and rides his gray mare Ticky Tack. I am the assistant trail captain.

We had twelve miles to come to our first camp. We stayed and dedicated the ruts where the Oregon Trail crosses the Little Blue River. We got into camp at 5 o'clock, it rained on us all day. The landowner's family prepared a supper for us and the governor of Missouri presented a proclamation and Missouri State Flag. The flag was taken off the capitol building and the

Missouri State Police brought it to the Kansas line where the Kansas State Police transported it on to us at our camp.

BK May 3. We left camp at 5 o'clock, it rained hard all night. We had thirty-three miles to cross to get through Kansas City. We got to Gardner, Kansas, at 6 o'clock and stayed at the fairgrounds. We have barns to put our horses in.

BK May 4. We left Gardner, Kansas, at 8 o'clock and are headed for our next camp at Hesper. Where the Santa Fe Trail branched off we had a dedication. There were several TV and news reporters there. We had a young man from Cheyenne, Wyoming, along. He was walking the Santa Fe Trail. We separated there. He took off down the Santa Fe Trail. We are continuing toward Oregon.

From Independence, the south route crossed the Blue River about fifteen miles out. Emigrants found many wagon trails leading to Westport. Their trail then went west to present Gardner, Kansas.

For those travelers who headed to Oregon from Westport, Shawnee Mission represented the last organized town and "civilization." At Trail Junction the Santa Fe trace continued southwest while the Oregon route turned right, generally northwest, in a line roughly parallel to the Wakarusa River and then the Kansas or Kaw River. It was at this point that the Oregon Trail became a separate route.

The House Committee on Roads, in 1925, reported: "There are two great trails in the history of America—the Santa Fe and the Oregon. Both of them left Independence, Mo., then followed the same track for 40 miles to where Gardner, Kansas, is now located, where the Santa Fe veered to the southwest and the Oregon to the northwest. At the forks was a sign, 'Road to Oregon.'"

*"Westport Landing" by William Henry Jackson. Westport, on the Missouri River near present-day Kansas City was a launching point for both the Santa Fe and Oregon Trails.* (Courtesy Scotts Bluff National Monument)

In 1806 Zebulon Pike headed west from St. Louis, following the Missouri and Kansas Rivers to the upper reaches of the Arkansas River. When he first spied the lofty peaks of the Rocky Mountain range, he said he would go to the highest one. Pike didn't reach that peak, but he eventually headed southwest to Santa Fe.

Upon returning home the Army lieutenant wrote about his journey, and the rich Spanish cities he found in the Southwest, foremost among them Santa Fe. Pike's writings spurred American interest in trading with the Spanish. In 1821 the Santa Fe Trail exploration by William Becknell opened the region. The Santa Fe Trail followed the Kansas River west from Independence, stretching across the length of present-day Kansas to reach the upper stretches of the Arkansas River.

The Santa Fe Trail split in present western Kansas. The earliest route headed slightly northwest into present-day Colorado, before turning southwest to cross the rugged Raton Pass. Having been used fairly regularly by traders since 1825, the Santa Fe Trail was a well-worn pathway when Oregon Trail emigrants started their journey.

**Ben Kern:**

BK May 5. We left Hesper on our way to camp at Eudora. At noon we stopped at a farmer's place. He let us go down through his hay fields on the ruts of the Oregon Trail. The ruts were a faint trace in the grass and we came near the original Little Blue River crossing, but couldn't ford because the east bank is washed out and too steep. There hasn't been anything across it for years. The west bank has a more gradual slope and we could see the ruts where the emigrants left the riverbed on their way west. We dedicated the crossing of the Little Blue River by placing a trail marker, one of the official Oregon Trail symbols used by the Oregon-California Trails Association to mark the route

We got into Eudora early, so we came on to Lawrence and camped at the fairgrounds here. A Cherokee Indian fellow came to the barns and shod some of the horses for us. He is a good shoer and has a stool so he can sit down to shoe the horses. He teaches at the Indian College. It has been raining all the time from Independence and the humidity is high. When we first got to Kansas some of the people said some farmers didn't get their hay up last year because of the rain. The country looks nice and green because of all the rain.

BK May 6. We left Lawrence for Big Spring. It rained hard, and there were tornado watches. We camped at the Bud Newell place. He raises horses so had a place for our horses. There were severe tornado warnings. One was real close so we had to take

*The wagon train had many rivers to cross between Missouri and Oregon.* (Bill White Photo)

cover. It rained, thundered, and lightninged all night long and we didn't get much sleep. We stayed in the garage all night.

BK May 7. We left for Topeka, the capital of Kansas. It was still raining when we got to the city limits of Topeka and a mounted state patrolman led us to the Capitol. We had lunch on the capitol steps, and the governor gave us a proclamation and a Kansas flag. We are camped at the Kansas Museum of History, which is a large place. We will stay here for three days.

The Cherokee we met a few days ago came to shoe Tom and Jerry. It was the first shoeing for those two and they had to be put in the shoeing stocks and were difficult to shoe. The stocks are like a chute. It is portable and you put each animal in and tie his head down. A piece of wide belting goes under his belly and you can lift the animal up off of his feet before putting the shoes on him. We had to do this in an underground maintenance room at the museum, because of the tornados. There were tornado watches every day, and we took the livestock to the maintenance room under the museum for safety.

I hooked Tom and Jerry one day while in Topeka. Eric, one of the support crew, was holding their heads as I hooked the team to the wagon. I was wearing my yellow slicker as I got up on the wagon seat. Tom looked back over the top of his blinds and could see my slicker and it spooked him. I didn't have my lines gathered up and wasn't even in the seat when the mules ran off with me. Eric had to jump out of the way so they wouldn't run over him. Tom and Jerry ran over one of the tipis and went up the ramp and across the patio in front of the museum. There were people everywhere and I was so glad not to have run over somebody in the big run away.

BK May 11. We left Topeka. I am driving the mules full time. I use a foot rope, called a Running W, on Tom in case he decides to run off again. If Tom tries to run, I can jerk the foot rope and trip him to slow him down. We got to Silver Lake early this afternoon and it is still raining. The rain is getting hard to take. Our cook quit at Topeka so we are looking for another cook.

Many people rode with Ben as he crossed Kansas and most had questions about him, the team he drove, and the country. One visitor asked what a couple of large grain silos on the route were used for. Ben, tired of the soaking rains replied, "Oh them, they're Kansas rain gauges."

The rains deluged the region. As rivers in the Midwest broke levees and dikes and poured over their banks, the nation's midsection saw its worst floods in decades. Thousands of people lost their homes as the torrential rains continued through

*Ben Kern was ready to go each morning, whether his team was mules or horses.* (Candy Moulton Photo)

May, June, and July. President Bill Clinton declared much of the region a disaster area.

As Ben crossed Kansas, he often saw ground that was once planted to corn or wheat that has now been returned to native grasses. The federal government had a program that allowed farmers to take crops out of production and receive a payment. Such "set-aside" lands couldn't be used for crops or livestock grazing, so often the native grasses reclaimed the soil either naturally or because farmers planted seed. That kept the soil from blowing away.

**Ben Kern:**

BK May 12. We are bound for St. Marys. This was a day long trip. The community cooked supper for us. A lady made a Guardian Angel for each of the wagons. I tied mine to the front bow of my wagon.

BK May 13. We left camp, crossed the Kaw River and stopped at the Big Elm, which is a famous landmark. The tree there is one hundred feet tall and twenty feet around. It has been hit by lightning several times. There is a lot of corn grown in this area.

BK May 14. We are off to Westmoreland. A wagon from Aurora, Oregon, joined us here and they have a real nice team of mules, Sue and Ann. Earl Leggett is the driver. Uncle Bill from Oregon plays the fiddle. We built a big fire and Uncle Bill and Ray played the music. We had a great party and a lot of fun.

The Aurora wagon started following the trail after the sesquicentennial train left Missouri. The Aurora community decided to have a wagon join the train as part of the trail's 150-year anniversary celebration. The mission of the wagon was to recreate the historic journey of the founder of Aurora Colony.

In the 1850s Dr. Wilhelm (William) Keil emigrated to Oregon where he founded a communal society, known as Aurora Colony. Originally located in Bethel, Missouri, Dr. Keil's colony believed in communal property, but decided to head west due to unrest over the Mormon issues, the instability due to slavery in the south, and other regional conflicts.

In 1854 the first delegation selected a settlement site at Willapa Bay, one hundred and twenty-five miles northwest of Portland. By May 1855 the Keil party was ready to depart for

*Earl Leggett, with the Aurora wagon, re-enacted the journey which carried Willie Keil's casket from Missouri to Oregon.* (Bill White Photo)

Oregon. Shortly before the travelers were to leave, Keil's eldest son, Willie, died of malaria. Dr. Keil had promised Willie he would take him to Oregon, so he kept his promise by having a special lead-lined coffin built. Dr. Keil placed the coffin holding Willie's body inside the first wagon and then filled the coffin with alcohol. Willie led the way west.

Upon arrival at Willapa Bay, Dr. Keil found that the site really didn't suit his colony. The climate was wet and heavily timbered. Although oysters filled the bay, no market existed for their exportation. Dr. Keil ultimately decided to move the colony to a new site, twenty-nine miles south of Portland. Named Aurora Mills, for one of Dr. Keil's daughters, the colony flourished in the Willamette Valley; it later moved a couple of miles south of the initial settlement and dropped the "Mills" to become simply Aurora.

As Earl Leggett recalled his journey in 1993 he said:

EL We pulled out of Independence by ourselves and caught up with [the other wagons in] Westmoreland, Kansas. We called the trip 'Bringing Willie Home.' Our wagon was built in 1880 by the Moline Plow and Implement Company. It was actually used in Aurora to deliver supplies to the old Aurora Colony Hotel. We painted it the original color to make the trip. The historical society let us take the wagon out of the museum for this purpose.

PULLED BY THE MULES Ann and Sue this wagon became the last in the train heading west in 1993. One of the Reed wagons dropped out so the girls could trade off driving. That meant the Aurora wagon had the fifth position in the train line—Ben's wagon led the way, followed by three wagons driven by the Reed girls, and the Aurora wagon was next. When additional wagons joined the train for short stints they fell into line after the Aurora wagon.

Earl recalled his early days with the team this way:

EL We wanted mules for the simple reason that Willie Keil's wagon had been pulled with a team of mules. If we was going to do something we was going to do it as authentically as we possibly could.

Sue and Ann were half sisters, five years old. I bought them for the Chamber of Commerce in Aurora, traded for them over the phone with a gentleman from Morganfield, Kentucky. They'd been together since they were colts, they trusted one another. We paid half up front, and the other half on delivery. Got money by donations and gifts.

I went to Kentucky to bring them to Independence and worked them in Morganfield for a couple of days. It took probably a good month and a half or so on the trail until we got to the point that I gained their trust, where they'd believe in me. There was times when they were skittish and all. Everyday there was something new. You had to really be on top of them.

We was in Kentucky to work 'em out. They had plowed, but [the owner] had never used them on an iron-wheeled wagon, so the first half day that I was there I adjusted all the harness and everything, which was brand new. I took two different kind of bits. Used a snaffle bit, working them on a rubber-tired wagon, and they were fine, that's all they'd ever had in their mouth. The next morning I said I would put them on the iron-wheeled wagon, and see if it bothered them any. So I was working them that afternoon. Worked probably twenty to twenty-four miles that day.

I was headed toward the house and turned off the hard road then headed up the gravel road toward the barn, about a quarter mile up the road from the house…and all the sudden they decided it was time to go home. A mule is different than a horse, they're gonna try you and so we went down the road just a flying. I worked the lines trying to get their heads back. My dad always taught me a runaway is something you never never bring home.

The wagon was just going down the road behind them, just a whiplashing behind them. The harder they run, the more noise the wagon made and the more it scared them…. My arms were about numb, but I wouldn't let 'em turn to the barnyard, I made them go on down the road. Got them stopped and they were just stepping up and down and I could tell it was time for them to go home.

There was no room to turn around there, but we turned around there anyway. We were fortunate that no cars or anything come down this country road. As soon as we got turned around I could just see they were going to go again, headed toward the barn. We stopped and started as we made our way to the barn. But when we got to the gate of the barnyard they took off. Around and around the barnyard they went. It was a big barnyard. It looked like the Pendleton chuckwagon races. You couldn't see the barn, you couldn't see the gate for the dirt and dust. The wagon was just careening around the yard.

I told them, "You're either going to stop or I'm going to break your necks" and we headed toward the barn. They got up to the barn and they stopped on a dime. It was a test that we was going through, whether I was going to get excited.

They sense if you're scared or not, a mule really does. They're smart. I said to them, "I haven't got time to be messing with this." The next morning I put different bits on them. We never had any big problems after that.

I was born and raised on a farm in West Virginia. Learned to drive teams as a kid. I used to ride along with Dad, then he put me on my own team and plow. Of course it was a place to babysit me more than anything else. I mowed and used to pull hay rakes, or haul hay on the wagons.

For Earl joining the sesquicentennial wagon train was just like it'd been in 1843. A wagon train was traveling down the trail and someone signed up with them. Earl told the story this way:

EL It was an unknown factor. We didn't know anybody. We paid to sign on and to travel the trip with a wagon boss, and we had to build a trust with and friendship with the people that were there already. I tried my best to build that rapport and build a trust and friendship with the people that were there.

Some people you can read right away and some you can't.

*A yoke of oxen stands hitched to a wagon at Rock Creek Station, Nebraska. Most early travelers on the Oregon Trail used oxen to pull their wagons. Gold-seekers headed toward California after 1849 most often used mules because they could travel more quickly than oxen did. Few early travelers relied on horses to pull their wagons.* (Candy Moulton Photo)

In Kansas when I signed on I could tell by Ben's handshake, there wasn't nothing phoney in Ben.

BEN KERN:

BK May 15. We pulled camp for Blue Rapids and it is still raining. I think everybody went out and ate dinner at a restaurant tonight just because we are tired of the rain. We were on the Oregon Trail ruts a lot this day on our way to Blue Rapids.

BK May 16. We left camp for Marysville and stopped at Alcove Springs. This is a historical spot. There was a big spring and waterfall and historically many people put their names on

*Earl Leggett, left, and Ben Kern, right, became good friends while driving teams pulling covered wagons over the Oregon Trail from Missouri to Oregon.* (Barbara Gaitley Photo)

the rocks. There is a grave site there where a little girl had died. Finally the sun shined and it did not even rain. At Marysville we camped at the Pony Express Park. We will lay over a day.

BK May 18. We are bound for Hanover. The folks cooked a big supper for us.

BK May 19. Left Hanover real early had 11 miles to go to meet the Nebraska wagon train at noon. We had a ceremony and met the Governor of Nebraska. Dedicated a monument and then came on to Odell to make camp.

BK May 20. The town's people of Odell put on a supper for the wagon train last night and cooked breakfast for us. We left Odell at 5 A.M. as we have 25 miles to Rock Creek Station.

Rock Creek is a historical place, one of the few Pony Express stations left, a lot of the buildings still standing. The barns and corrals, the well house, watering trough, and the telegraph office.

BK May 21. We camped overnight at Rock Creek. This morning we came back to Odell to lay over here for five days.

BK May 22–26. We have panels for corrals for our horses and the townspeople of Odell furnished the feed for our livestock. One night they put on a barbecue and a street dance. We put new brakes on our wagons and done repairs. Shod some of our horses, whose shoes had worn thin from the gravel roads. Larry and wife that owned the local restaurant cooked breakfast for us every morning. We made a lot of good friends while in Odell.

BK May 27. We left Odell to join up with the Nebraska train again. We will travel with that state-sanctioned train until we reach Wyoming.

**ROCK CREEK STATION to FORT KEARNY**

Progression of the 1993 Sesquicentennial Wagon Train

PART TWO:

# *Rock Creek Station to Fort Kearny*

*Had a taste of som turtle meat which some of the boys caught after we camped last knight which was quite a treat.*

—EDWIN BIRD, MAY 18, 1854

ROCK CREEK STATION, NEBRASKA. Tall grasses and short bushes at Rock Creek Station in extreme southeastern Nebraska mark Oregon Trail ruts that are fifty to sixty feet wide and five to six feet deep. Wagons passing Rock Creek from 1843 to 1866 ground the clay surface into talcum dust. Erosion created the trail ruts.

Trails cross Nebraska like tributaries on a river. The various routes join in central Nebraska at Fort Kearny. Trail ruts are plainly visible at Rock Creek Station, but most of east and central Nebraska is rolling farmland, green or golden with corn, wheat, alfalfa, and soybeans. There the trail is plowed under rich soil.

Just as Ben made wagon repairs at Rock Creek, other earlier emigrants did the same. William Riley Franklin headed west in 1850 and wrote in his journal:

WRF ∩ Wed. [April] 15th. We elected to lay by to rest our animals, have some of our wagons repaired, wash and etc. A group of the younger men decided to go on a buffalo hunt while we were resting. They did not have the proper equipment,

*An old well site frames a Pony Express marker embedded in a large stone at Rock Creek Station, near Fairbury, Nebraska.* (Candy Moulton Photo)

or organization but so equipped and prepared, they set off. The buffalo soon hove in sight. And so as might be expected (without a commander), they made a fruitless charge—fired several guns, to no effect. The buffalo soon scampered off at a proper and practicable distance (for their safety and comfort) from the young enthusiastic hunters.

IN 1854 EDWIN Ruthven Bird headed west from Naperville, Illinois. Soon after leaving he remarked on the Indians and the missions: "Thursday May 11th. The Tribes of Indians we have passed through are the Shawneas & Potawatameas. The latter have several misinaries among them." Farther west, in Nebraska, he noted they camped in the "hunting country of the Caw Indians."

Today members of those tribes, and others of the plains, are settled in cities and towns, or on reservations far from their native homelands. Emigrants first displaced the Indians, at least in part because the movement of so many wagons over the land caused buffalo and other game animals to stay away from the migration corridor. Later the military forced Native Americans to relinquish their tribal lands to allow not only emigrants, but also miners, to cross the region.

BEN KERN:

BK May 28. At camp along Rock Creek we saw lots of wild turkeys and could hear them gobbling in the grass both last evening and this morning. We left our camp in the big, old oak trees at Rock Creek State Historical Park. Our wagons went up the deep ruts of the Oregon Trail through the fresh, tall spring grasses. We had a good reception when we got to Fairbury. Paraded through town. Lots of people to meet us. Fairbury is a really old town. Cobblestone streets and real old buildings. The town's people cooked supper for us.

BK May 29. Left Fairbury for Alexandra Lakes. Rained all day. About an hour before we got to camp we had a Cloud Burst. Never seen so much water. Had a hard time making camp. Had a downpour all night long.

BK May 30. Left for our next camp at Deshler. Still raining. We camped about 6 miles out of Deshler on a ranch. The people of Deshler came out and gave us a barbecue.

*"Rock Creek Station" by William Henry Jackson. Located near present-day Endicott, Nebraska, this site was a favored stop on the Oregon Trail and also served as a Pony Express station.* (Courtesy Scotts Bluff National Monument)

BK May 31. Left Deshler real early after the townspeople came and cooked our breakfast. Have a lot of miles to go today. The roads are really muddy. Our support crew is having a hard time getting around. Lots of red dobie in this part of the country. This part of the country is really showing the effects of all the rain. Got to Oak at 6 o'clock. Farmers can't get into their fields to do work because it is so wet and muddy.

Our support crew travels in pickups. Sometimes we've had six or eight people in that crew. They tear down camp when we leave each morning, then travel, usually on paved roads, to the next campsite where they put up the two big tipis and smaller tents. They put out picket lines for the horses, and the cook makes our dinner. When we arrive, camp is set, so we can unhitch our teams, feed them, then relax or eat our own dinner.

EARL LEGGETT:

EL I have a canvas top, but I chose not to put it all the way up on the first bow for the simple fact that it absolutely makes me blind, you have no sight to the right or left of you. I moved that canvas back intentionally. It leaves me setting right out in the weather: rain, hail, wind, sun. It all bears down on my head.

Edwin Bird wrote on May 17, 1854:

EB 1854. This morning found an Ox ded is supposed to choaked in the yoak It has been cloudy all day with a strong cold north easter To soil being sandy & clayly the dust flew considerable not with standing the recent heavy rains I have been chilley all day & this eavning have considerable feaver took som composition which Mrs Tomas of Naperville gave me & retired to my tent early The country we have passed through is very handsom

Thursday 18th. This morning I feel much better. Had a taste of som turtle meat which some of the boys caught after we camped last knight which was quite a treat.

BEN KERN:

BK June 1. Left Oak to our next camp at Deweese, got into camp early. They had a Big Feed for us—grilled pork chops and lots of homemade pies. I had gone to bed when Dave Makeg came by to wake me up. He said Tom was down with colic. I went to check on him, got him up, and started walking him. We called a vet out of Hastings. It took him a long time to get here. These guys from the bar across the street come over and we took turns walking Tom. The walking is necessary to ease the mule's pain and keep him from lying down and rolling, which can twist a gut and make him die. The vet got here about midnight. He gave Tom a shot and later stuck a needle in his side. We loaded him and hauled him to the vet's clinic in Hastings.

*Mark and Mike, Ben's team.* (Ben Kern Photo)

BK June 2. Tom died early this morning. This was a sad day for me. He had become a very good mule. We left camp late. Everybody felt Bad about Tom. I started driving Mark and Mike again, the team I started driving at Independence. Arrived at Lone Tree Station late in the evening.

EARL LEGGETT:

EL I hated it when we lost Tom, I'd heard how Ben broke them and everything. It was a loss for him and on the morning Tom died, Ben didn't have to say anything, I could tell he was hurting and it took him a while to get over it. Jerry she was lost, even though Tom picked on her all the time. She was lost. You seen her attitude change. Animals got their own feelings, too.

BEN KERN:

BK June 3. Left camp for Dyer Park on the Little Blue

River. The community fed the wagon train people supper. They had an Oregon Trail program and a band. This is a big grassy area and lots of trees.

BK June 4. 8:00 left for our next camp at Kenesaw. Real friendly community. Put us up at the fire station. Cooked supper and breakfast for us. We parked our wagons on the main street.

BK June 5. Left Kenesaw for Minden, Nebraska. We had lunch at the little town of Heartwell. The bicycle tour that is retracing the Oregon Trail had lunch with us. Heartwell people fixed lunch for us, gave us cookies. I got a chocolate cake a lady gave to me, a big chocolate cake. Came on to Minden to the fairgrounds. We're going to lay over here a day. Went though the museum here at Minden, it is really interesting. Lots of history here.

BK June 6. Last night we had real bad tornado warning and the most severe lightning storm I have ever seen. I think all stayed up and watched all night.

BK June 7. We left Minden for Fort Kearny, our next campsite. When we got into camp we found out that a rancher across the river from the Fort lost 30 head of cattle from the tornado last night. Fort Kearny is a good place to camp. Big area and lots of trees.

BK June 8. Dave and Whitey Bowhay signed up with the wagon train. One of their mares had a colt tonight. Fort Kearny had lots of festivities, dancers, a band, and local people served meals.

EARL LEGGETT:

EL We watched the tornadoes go by and the next day we could see the route that we took was right where the tornadoes went. I never felt in real danger. I'd been born and raised in West Virginia, they have cyclones and flash floods. If the animals are loose and free they'll take care of themselves. There's not a lot you can do other than find a place to lay down and get away from it. No sense running from them. I'd go to sleep, the rest of the people, some of the people on the wagon train would be up watching them.

Between four hundred and eight hundred wagons with up to ten thousand animals passed Spring Ranch on the Little Blue River east of Pauline, every day during the Oregon migration. As emigrants crossed the prairie they died of accidents and disease. Asiatic Cholera killed the most emigrants in Nebraska as the people drank stagnant water and entire families died. Estimates of the number of people who died vary, but most historians agree about one in every seventeen people who started west died before completing the journey. A conservative average, according to Merrill Mattes in *The Great Platte River Road*, estimates about ten graves for every mile of trail. Most agree to an estimate of at least four graves to a mile between St. Joseph, commonly called St. Joe, and Fort Laramie. However, between Fort Kearny and the forks of the Platte River graves sat only about two hundred feet apart.

As the migrants followed the Little Blue and Platte Rivers, the water moved slowly. It became a breeding ground for bacteria that caused daily death. Dysentery and cholera could kill a person in a matter of a few hours as it brought on sudden, profuse diarrhea leading to rapid dehydration.

The trek from the Blue to the Platte River—about fifty miles—was the longest stretch in Nebraska that the historic Oregon-bound travelers were without any water. However, much longer stretches existed between sources of good, clean water. The party Ben traveled with hauled water for the animals on a flatbed trailer in a large plastic tank. Periodically they drained the tank and washed it out with chlorine bleach to kill any bacteria and germs.

The train traveled with another flatbed trailer equipped with two portable bathrooms, which could be used when necessary. The modern-day travelers didn't have to rely on a clump of grass or a rare tree for privacy. And the women didn't need to use their full skirts for cover.

Near Hastings Susan Hail died on her way west. One story is that on June 2, 1852, she drank from a spring poisoned by Indians and the thirty-four-year-old woman died with alarming suddenness. It is more likely the water she drank came from a source too close to the campground, or a buffalo wallow, and was therefore unsafe.

Hail's newlywed husband, heartbroken, walked back to St. Joe where he bought a tombstone and a wheelbarrow. He pushed the one-wheeled implement back to the site of her lonely grave northwest of Kenesaw and placed the marker on her burial site. Ironically, though the story of her death and his dedication passed through the years, no details survive about the husband, not even his name.

Fort Kearny, located on bottomland south of the Platte near the upper end of the "Grand Island" in the Platte, was the first fort built to protect travelers on the Oregon Trail. It remained garrisoned from 1848 to 1871.

The military built an earlier Fort Kearny in 1846 at the Missouri River, which is now the site of Nebraska City. However, that fort wasn't set on the primary migration route and emigrants needed protection farther west, so the military moved the fort.

Lieutenant Daniel P. Woodbury chose the new site. In the spring of 1848, he and 175 men started making adobe blocks for construction of the fort, then called Fort Child in honor of Brigadier General Child. Other buildings were of logs from the islands of the Platte River and sod from the prairie. The fort's name was later changed to honor General Stephen Watts Kearny.

A *New York Herald* correspondent passed the area in 1857 and 1858 and wrote this account of Fort Kearny:

NYH ∩ 1857. The fort consists of five unpainted wooden houses, two dozen long, low mud buildings. The houses are built around a large open square or parade ground.... Trees have been set out along the borders of the parade ground, and they are the only bushes that can be seen in any direction except a few straggling ones on the banks of the Platte a few miles distant.

LARGE COTTONWOOD trees now line the perimeter of Fort Kearny, and stone markers on the northwest corner mark the Oregon Trail. Some of the original buildings are restored and used for displays prepared by the Nebraska State Parks Division. Costumed guides interpret the history of Fort Kearny, which is enclosed with a wire fence. During its period of military use, the fort had no fortifications.

Joshua D. Breyfogle wrote May 8, 1849, "We arrived at Fort Kearney after noon. Here we had an opportunity of sending letters to our friends. The officers are going to send a mail to the States in the morning and kindly offered to transmit any letter we wished to send."

The military abandoned Fort Kearny in 1871 and a few years later the military reservation was thrown open to settlement. Later a community grew on the north side of the river, which took the name Kearney, using a different spelling than the fort.

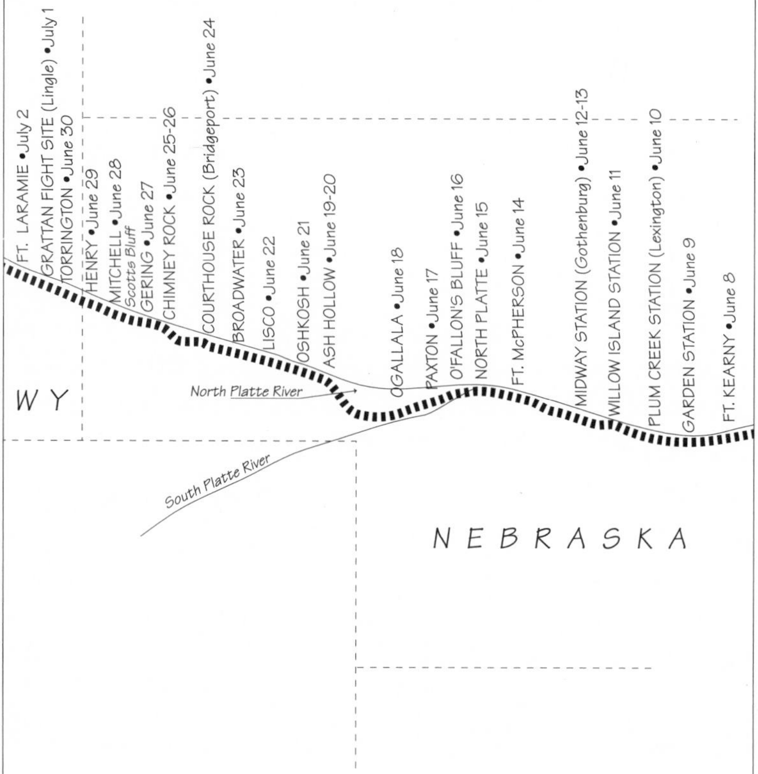

FT. LARAMIE •July 2
GRATTAN FIGHT SITE (*Lingle*) •July 1
TORRINGTON •June 30
HENRY •June 29
MITCHELL •June 28
*Scotts Bluff*
GERING •June 27
CHIMNEY ROCK •June 25-26
COURTHOUSE ROCK (*Bridgeport*) •June 24
BROADWATER •June 23
LISCO •June 22
OSHKOSH •June 21
ASH HOLLOW •June 19-20
OGALLALA •June 18
PAXTON •June 17
O'FALLON'S BLUFF •June 16
NORTH PLATTE •June 15
FT. McPHERSON •June 14
MIDWAY STATION (*Gothenburg*) •June 12-13
WILLOW ISLAND STATION •June 11
PLUM CREEK STATION (*Lexington*) •June 10
GARDEN STATION •June 9
FT. KEARNY •June 8

WY

North Platte River

South Platte River

NEBRASKA

**FORT KEARNY to FORT LARAMIE**

Progression of the 1993 Sesquicentennial Wagon Train

PART THREE:

# *Fort Kearny to Fort Laramie*

*The turtles were laying their eggs*
*and building their nests right along the river.*
—Earl Leggett, 1993

Fort Kearny, Nebraska. Like a braided strand of hair, many emigrant roads came into Fort Kearny from the east, but from that point west, there was just one main trail, although at times it had many parallel pathways, formed when the wagons fanned apart to avoid dust and to find feed for their stock.

Ben Kern:

BK June 9. We left Fort Kearny headed for Garden Station. We got up to the south side of the Platte River and had dinner today and came into Garden Station. Got into here about 4 o'clock. Staying on private property. Real good weather today. Passed the Plum Creek Massacre site.

We read a marker that said this area was part of a coordinated attack by the Sioux, Cheyenne, and Arapaho ranging from Julesburg, Colorado, eastward, during 1865. The Indians, in retaliation for the November 1864 Sand Creek Massacre by Colonel John Chivington, attacked cabins and wagons. Men, women and children died in the retaliatory attacks in Nebraska and some were taken prisoner including Mrs. T.F. Morton, who was captured in the area we passed through today. Mrs. Morton and several of the other captives later were ransomed in the Powder River country of Wyoming and were turned over to authorities at the Platte Bridge Station in July of 1865.

BK Today's the 10th of June. We left Garden Station headed for Lexington at the Plum Creek Station. Real good weather today, real warm today. Got in about 3:30.

BK June 11. We left Lexington, Plum Creek Station, we headed for Willow Island Station out of Cozad. Warm again today and we done about 22 miles today. Got in about 4:30.

OREGON TRAIL travelers in 1993 didn't fear attacks by renegade whites or Indians, but they saw a repeat of some natural situations encountered by earlier emigrants.

In 1854 Edwin Bird wrote:

EB 1854 Monday 15 [May]. About one oclock this morning a heavy Thunderstorm came upon us & lasted untill day break had a tuff time with the stock They stampeded four or five times A purson who never saw Catle in this wonderful feat would be surprized & somewhat frightened In such time most all of the men are on gard chosing to brest the storm in the tents rather than be run over and probably killed The drove were formed in a circle & the guard around them all would be still & quiet & dark as pitch excepting as very often was the case a streak of lightning would reveal the compact living mass then would follow the deafning bolt then look wild in an instance the catle would drop or croach to the earth & rising would start in a solid body & go like wild fire over rocks through raviuns & off the pararies

EB Tuesday 16th. Last knight it did rain sure enough & a Thunder Storm of the first magnatude The wind changed sixteen times blowing hard all the while The catle stampeded all knight but we were prepared all being on horse back we cep them in a circle where once & a while they would fairly hum There was one constant blace of lightning & roar of thunder.... To knight we are wet our blankets are in the saim situation While the ground we are to lay on is wet wetter confoundadly wet An there is not the least spark of fire to warm us by.

Ben Kern added his perspective:

BK —June 12, Saturday. Real bad storm hit us about 4:30 this morning, lots of thunder and lightning, and it rained really really bad. We're gonna leave here about 8 o'clock and we're headed for Midway Station at Gothenburg. In the night, Buck got me up and said there's a storm a coming. And it hit. I was laying in my camper and every time the lightning would hit I could see the horses pulling on the picket line and I thought they were going to pull it over.

Buck headed back for his camper. He seen this streak going across the meadow and it was this Australian. He was camped in one of those little old tents with just room enough to crawl into. Joe Vogel slept in the Nebraska Wagon, a big company wagon. You could zip up the back end of it. The Australian just went through the canvas and landed in there with Joe. That guy was scared, he said "we don't have that kind of stuff in Australia."

We traveled with the Nebraska state wagon train. Their wagons and ours were used to give people rides, if they wanted to pay a fee to join us for the day. Usually we charged $125 each day, but Nebraska only charged $15, so we cut our rates, too. We also had some extra horses that we rented to people who wanted to ride with us.

It's stopped raining now. We stopped at a ranch and had dinner and we're heading now for the Pony Express Station.

We're here at the Midway Pony Express Station. Got in here at 2:30. We're going to mail some mail out, the Pony Express is going to carry it. The Pony Express brought our mail out yesterday, I got two letters. We had a pretty good celebration at the station. We left about 3:00, got into Gothenburg about 4:30 and camped there. Will lay over a day.

BK June 13. Went out to a German Fest last night, had a real big feed. Had a pretty bad storm last night, the wind blowed, had lots of lightning.

BK June 14. We left Gothenburg at 7 this morning and we're heading for Fort McPherson. We got a 31 mile day today. We usually average between 18–20 miles on the road.

We just went by a place where the Oregon Trail crossed the Platte River from the south side to the north side, where the old original trail was. Between Gothenburg and McPherson we were headed north and we came right down to the Platte River and followed right along the river. We were on a gravel road and where we made a bend in the road, a hundred yards from the river, we could see the old original wagon ruts. They looked like a big swale dropping into the river. The tracks went down between the willows and not far from the trail ruts was a real old house, where somebody came and took a homestead.

BK June 15. We got into McPherson last night about 4 o'clock and camped there and we left there this morning about 8. We're headed for North Platte. We're going by a spot here in the Sandhills called Sioux Point. It's about four miles out of McPherson and it was a lookout for the Indians to watch the wagon trains. We had lunch here just under Sioux Point. We got in to North Platte here about 3:30 and we're camped here at the college campus.

THERE IS A GOUGED trail from the road to the top of Sioux Point, worn by the tennis shoes and hiking boots of area residents and tourists, who want to see the view from the top. Trail ruts are more visible in western Nebraska where the land hasn't been turned to corn. Near North Platte the terrain becomes mostly hills with cedar trees.

One story of the early trail is that people didn't need a guide. They could follow the route by the smell of dead animals. By 1858 "the traveler could find his way with no other compass to guide than his nose alone," emigrant Kirk Knox said.

BEN KERN:

BK This is June the 16th. We left North Platte at 7 o'clock this morning, the North and South Platte Rivers make a fork here, and we will follow the North fork. We're headed for O'Fallon's Bluff, we're going to camp there by a big lake. We're going to go through some of the old ruts that are like a really rugged two-track road with sandy spots that make travel particularly difficult. Vehicles can't go through this area. We're halfway between North Platte and O'Fallon's Bluff and we stopped here at Down's ranch, real big lot, and we're having dinner here. Wind blowing real hard today.

BK June 17. Got into O'Fallon's Bluff last night about 4:30. Camped by the lake. Real big storm came in last night, but it blowed over. Left O'Fallon's Bluff this morning at 7 o'clock, We're headed for Paxton. We're stopped now for a potty break, pulled in here to a pasture and we're pretty close to the interstate.

BK June 18. Left our camp this morning at 7. Crossed the South Platte River. Went through Paxton and we're headed to Ogallala. Stormed last night, rained quite a bit, pretty cool and cloudy today. We stopped at a ranch and had lunch. Left there about noon and we got into Ogallala to the fair grounds and we're gonna camp here for the night.

CANDY MOULTON:

CM An all-night soaking rain turned the ground in Ogallala to mud the first night I joined the wagon train as a reporter for the *Casper Star-Tribune*. As Ben harnessed the next morning clouds lay low upon the ground forming a gray curtain above us. Tom Westerbuhr of Wilcox, Nebraska, watched. "I always did like good horses," he told me, as he waited to ride the Nebraska wagon for a day. A retired farmer, Tom once drove wagons full of grain from his family farm to the nearest town nine miles away.

Bill Russell of Rocksburg, Kansas, told me he had been on the wagon train since the Kansas-Nebraska border. He planned to ride at least to Wyoming and perhaps farther. "Despite the modern day era that we live in, we've been able to re-create in our minds... the era of the pioneer," he said.

The transcontinental railroad completed in 1869 negated the real need for the Oregon Trail. During the night I had heard the rain and the rumble of the train passing through Ogallala, a main gathering point on the Texas Trail, where cowboys brought their herds to the railroad shipping point.

During the peak of the cattle drives some three hundred thousand head of Texas cattle passed through Ogallala every year. Some moved on north into Wyoming and Montana, but cowboys loaded others onto Union Pacific trains headed to eastern markets.

In all some ten million Texas cattle moved north during the period from 1865–1885, pushed by fifty thousand cowboys riding half a million horses. Although trail driving brought the

*"Crossing the South Platte" by William Henry Jackson. The trail was routed to avoid as many river crossings as possible. Often described as an inch deep and a mile wide, the Platte River could still pose problems during spring floods or with its hidden quicksands.* (Courtesy Scotts Bluff National Monument)

cattle north, it ceased after 1885 due to many factors, including approval of quarantine laws to halt the spread of fever carried by a tick on the Texas cattle, the settlement of much of the range by homesteader/nesters, and the invention of barbed wire. The homesteaders put fences around their land and around watering holes. The cattlemen could no longer easily drive herds from Texas because towns and barbed wire barricades blocked the trails. Overgrazing also affected both the range and the trails.

Also, severe winters in northern areas from 1885–1886 to 1887–1888 killed hundreds of thousands of head of stock in a period known as "The Big Die-Up." The great era of the western cattle trail dust was over and the rowdy, raucous cowtowns like Ogallala settled down as well.

When the wagon train camped in Ogallala, Union Pacific trains hauling coal and other freight sped by a few hundred yards from U.S. Highway 30, which the wagons used as a route. Interstate 80 crosses Nebraska not far to the south. The trains and the highways are main transportation corridors these days; people passed us in their pickups and cars, waving and pointing video cameras our way.

Speeding along at the double nickel—55 miles per hour—they sometimes seemed frustrated at our slow three-mile-per hour pace. I rode with Kris, a teen-aged chatterbox, who curtly told me how to climb aboard her wagon and where to sit. But she also flashed a huge grin as she lifted the warm folds of a tattered quilt that lay over her legs so that it covered mine as well.

As we drove, she talked of CFNBs. When I asked what that meant, she responded "Corn Fed Nebraska Boys." Her hands were swollen and cracked and dried blood flaked on her knuckles. The cornfields looked more like rice paddies, so much water stood in the rows. A light rain started falling and Kris and I slid as far to the right of the seat as possible seeking protection from the wagon covering. We pulled a brown plastic tarp over our ragged quilt as the horses continued their constant stepping.

I handled the lines for a while to give Kris a break and rest her arms. She has a tremendous set of muscles, developed while driving her team every day. Before long my own arms began to ache. My fingers crimped and cramped and I admitted to Kris that I was not a good driver as our wagon wove from side to side because I failed to keep the lines steady.

In 1843 travelers who were headed West sent messages back home to relatives with anyone they met going the opposite direction on the trail. Following in that oral tradition, some of this crew sent messages ahead to their homes and friends in Casper with the bus tourists they met in Brule. "Tell everybody in Casper we'll see them in a few days," Ben said, even though the train wouldn't be to Casper for almost a month.

Thirteen wagons and about seventy-five people traveled with the train that day. Some of them camped for the night at California Hill where they walked among the yellow flowering cactus and knee-high prairie grasses. The ruts are deep in the soil there, but it's difficult to distinguish those made by wagons and those struck by cattle as they trail over this native range.

Ben Kern:

BK June 19. California Hill is real steep. It was muddy, hard to pull, but we're up on top now heading out through the Sandhills. We stopped here for dinner, buffalo burgers and baked beans. We're getting ready to leave to head toward Ash Hollow.

To Ash Hollow at 4:30. There sure was a lot of people here to meet us. We're going to camp here today and lay over tomorrow. Looks like a real good camp spot.

BK June 20. We're going to lay over here today, and do some repairs and stuff. Real heavy dew on the grass this morning.

Earl Leggett:

EL On the trail my mules Sue and Ann give me a little trouble sometimes when the big tractor trailers and the big farm equipment comes zooming by... if they get surprised they want to shy toward the ditch. Ann... it seemed like the vibration from the iron wheels would just transfer to her and every now and then I really have to watch her for that. They don't like loud people.

West of Ogallala, Kingsley Dam holds the North Platte River backing its waters into Lake McConaughy. The Nebraska Sandhills stretch to the north and the countryside changes from flat farmland to rolling hills and cattle ranches.

There is more sage and prickly pear. When early-day government explorer Lieutenant Stephen Long passed over this land in 1820, he called it a desert and said it really wasn't much good for anything and certainly didn't appear habitable.

However, by the 1870s as homeseekers and would-be cattle barons looked for land, they soon realized the western prairies had an underground aquifer. They noticed that the bison which lived on the native buffalo and grama grasses had in places dug into the sandy soil to find water.

The land long labeled the "Great American Desert" became the homesteaders' and cattlemen's choice as they sought a place to sink roots. It is still cattle country, the sandy soil held in place by the native prairie grasses.

William Riley Franklin's birth took place in Franklin County, Kentucky, in 1825. He married Josephine Pryor in Missouri in 1848 and two years later left Clinton County, Missouri, for upper California to try his luck in the "gold diggins."

Like other Forty-Niners, Franklin's party traveled with good stock and moved quickly, making the trip across the country much more quickly than the Oregon emigrants. Bad weather plagued his party across eastern Nebraska. The condition of the land affected many travelers as they headed west. Early emigrants found the best forage for their livestock, but range conditions near the trail soon deteriorated.

In western Nebraska Franklin wrote about the rangeland:
WRF ∩ Camp 17 Tuesday 7th [May 1850]. To our left today and yesterday as far as the eye could see were buffalo ordure, resembling an old pasture that had been turned out where had been kept innumerable thousands of cattle for years. The grass and herbage of every kind is leveled with the ground. Scarcely a shelter for a mountain rabbit, and from the carcasses and bones

that are bleached and bleaching, one would suppose that it had been inhabited by buffalo ever since God spoke the world into existence.... South Platte is near half as wide as N. Platte.

WRF ∩ Camp 18 Wednesday 8th. We, this day after a march of 20 miles, encamped on the margin of the aforesaid river. Here we again found extensive forest of "prairie fuel" and tolerable good grazing, consequently we fared well and rested finely tonight.

WRF ∩ Camp 21, Saturday 11th. Our caravan progressed 18 miles up the river and encamped. Here we found very fine grazing etc. Today we received two more wagons into our train, increasing our caravan to 13 wagons and company to 50 men.

WRF ∩ Camp 22, Sunday 12th. After a march of 25 miles over a deep sandy road, we camped in sight of "Council Rock" near the river. Here we found very good gramma grass, is said to be very strong and nourishing, and is equal to Timothy hay. There is one thing certain, that if the grass here did not possess more strength and nutrition than our common prairie grass, it would not be possible for our animals to cross the plains, starting as soon as we did. There is here also a kind of gramma called Buffalo grass that is excellent flavor and good pasturage. This day we passed 3 graves side by side, who died last summer of cholera....

NEAR THE HEAD OF Ash Hollow upstream from Lake McConaughy, travelers faced Windlass Hill. Rolling over the prairie had been easy until that point where the travelers had to descend a three hundred foot hill at a twenty-five degree slope.

Windlass Hill, the very first steep hill emigrants encountered, made a profound impact on them and the land. They rough-locked the wheels of the wagons with chains to keep them from turning as they slid to the bottom. That process cut deeply into the hillside, tearing the vegetation away. Subsequent erosion left the hill with still-visible scars. The wagon wheels cut into the earth, and the ruts here are deep and lasting, made by the emigrants and retained, even enhanced, by the constant wash of wind and rain.

At Windlass Hill Captain Howard Stansbury, who was on an exploratory trip to the Great Salt Lake, wrote on July 3, 1852: HS ∩ 1852. Here we were obliged, from the steepness of the road, to let the wagons down by ropes, but the labor of a dozen men for a few days would make a descent easy and safe. The bottom of Ash Creek is tolerably well wooded, principally of ash and some dwarf cedars...traces of the great tide of emigration ...plainly visible in remains of camp fires, in blazed trees covered with innumerable names...total absence of all herbage.

It's unclear why it's called Windlass Hill. Historians agree there is no evidence to suggest emigrants used some type of windlass to lower wagons. If such a fixed contraption came into use on the hill, it was sometime after 1866, according to Mattes in *The Great Platte River Road.*

Windlass Hill drops into Ash Hollow where fine ash trees line the hillsides, giving the area its name. The presence of good water was a welcome relief for historic travelers as the North Fork of the Nebraska River cut through the bottom of the hollow, which also had a cold, crystal clear spring.

One emigrant wrote of traveling 140 miles before reaching Ash Hollow: "so much sickness and no good water."

In 1854 the Grattan Massacre took place near Fort Laramie. That incident involved a cow, Sioux Indians, and U.S. troops and preceded a battle west of Ash Hollow. On September 3, 1855, Sioux and soldiers clashed at Blue Water Creek near Ash Hollow.

*A chain such as this could be wrapped around the wagon wheels to form a rough-lock and keep the wheels from turning when going down steep hills. If trees were available travelers sometimes tied limbs to their wagon wheels to prevent turning, forming another type of rough-lock.* (Candy Moulton Photo)

"This has been a busy and exciting day for us but a bloody and disastrous one to the Sioux," Captain John B.S. Todd wrote September 3, 1855.

The fight resulted in the deaths of Indian men, women, and children, and the events became known as the Harney Massacre, named for Colonel W. S. Harney. It often is called the Bloody Blue Fight.

Some historians say the Bloody Blue Fight marked the beginning of the real conflict between Indians and the white men that ended with the battle on the Little Big Horn in 1876. Others claim it was the earlier Grattan Massacre in Wyoming that precipitated the Indian-military controversy. Since the two are directly linked, it makes little difference. After the Bloody Blue battle, tensions constantly escalated among travelers, the military, and the Indians.

Ben Kern:

BK June 21. We're going to leave camp here at Ash Hollow this morning and we're headed toward Oshkosh. We got in to camp at 3:30. We're about three miles southwest of Oshkosh.

BK June 22nd about 7 A.M. We're about ready to leave here. We're headed for Lisco. We're going to stay in the roping arena in Lisco today. Rained a little bit last night. We had dinner in a great big grove of cottonwood trees. We circled our wagons in a meadow where the grass touched our horses' bellies. They enjoyed the fresh feed as we ate our dinner. We got into Lisco about 2:30 and we're standing here now watching funnel clouds. One funnel cloud touched down and was kinda headed our way. We're watching another one, it's kind of southeast of Bridgeport. In all, three of them raced around our camp today.

BK This is June the 23rd at 7 A.M. We're getting ready to leave the roping arena here at Lisco and we're headed to Broadwater.

It's 2 o'clock now and we're just out of Broadwater a little ways and we're going right along the North Platte River, we're on the south side of the North Platte. We're about 8 miles out of Bridgeport. Got into a real bad storm, couple of tornadoes running, and it rained real hard and hailed a little bit, had to turn our wagons around. Had to get away from the wind and this storm. We got in to camp about 3:30, all soaking wet.

SCOTTSBLUFF STAR HERALD Farm Editor Mary Crawford rode with the wagons as the tornadoes tore across the Nebraska hills. She wrote: "At 2:50 [this] afternoon, riders had come back through the train spreading the alert. Morrill County was in a tornado watch and severe thunderstorm warning. We started to plan. If we spotted a tornado, go to the north ditch, pull the bridles off the horses, and maybe the saddles, too."

As the wagons reached the intersection of highways 382 and 92, southeast of Bridgeport, riders put on rain slickers and fastened the canvas covers down on the wagons. Crawford wrote: "There was NO protection from Mother Nature. She was in control. And she let her rains and hail descend."

The storm spooked the animals and the travelers. Some of the drivers unharnessed their animals. The people and the horses only wanted to put their backs toward the wind. "Minutes seemed like an hour," Crawford wrote.

EARL LEGGETT:

EL The worst probably 24-hour period we had was when we had the rain and then the five tornadoes and the next day when we had the rain and drove into the hail storm. A lot of the people had never been around situations like that. You can't just keep your animals standing there, they're gonna run on you. You got to keep moving. A lot of the people from Nebraska they pulled off in the corn fields and everything else. We stopped for a few minutes. I said, "We need to get moving on down the road because the animals are looking for something to do." We just went on down the road at a trot. We went on and 5 to 10 minutes later were out of it. It was rain and hail, caused from the tornadoes that we were going through.

BEN KERN:

BK June 24. We're going to backtrack about three miles,

and we're going to go into a place where I was born, circle the wagons, and take a few pictures.

[Later] we went by the old homestead where I was born. Went in and met with the land owners, Vi and Bob Newton, circled the wagons around the grove of trees, had a dedication and visited with the landowners quite a bit and came back out to the original trail again. We pulled the hill up here to Courthouse Rock and Jail Rock, we circled the wagons up here and are having lunch. It is about 1:30, quarter to 2. My cousin Joe Spear was standing alongside the road and he came up to the wagon and shook hands with me, first time I'd seen him in probably 20 years.

BK June 25. We're hooked up here and going to leave Bridgeport here about 7 o'clock. We're going to go to Chimney Rock today.

We got into Chimney Rock about 4:30 and made camp. When we got in the movie outfits were here, took some pictures, then we had to set up our camp.

SCOTT'S BLUFF IS AT THE upper end of the "Valley of the Monuments." The place provided visual sustenance for the pioneer. After the tedium and monotony of crossing the plains, the formations in western Nebraska were fantasy for the travelers.

In the natural rocks they saw courthouses, cathedrals and fortresses. Those formations became Courthouse Rock, Jail Rock, and Chimney Rock. Traveling by wagon, you see the landmark rocks long before you reach them. Like a beacon or a point of light they constantly draw you closer until eventually you stand near and make a shadow of your own.

"This rock is 200 feet high and can be seen at a distance of 20 miles and when seen from this distance it resembles some tall monument, erected on a well-contested battlefield in memory of

*Historic travelers watched Chimney Rock for days as they traveled toward the natural marker in Western Nebraska and nearly all of them made some mention of the sentinel in their journals and diaries. The 1993 sesquicentennial train camped near the landmark.* (Candy Moulton Photo)

the brave dead who sleep beneath its towering summit," William Riley Franklin wrote of Chimney Rock in May 1850.

EARL LEGGETT:

EL — You could see for miles and see Chimney Rock and Scotts Bluff coming for days. Before we got there it got to be the same old thing every day and every day. When we was going through there the turtles were laying their eggs and building their nests right along the river. They were big land turtles. They would dig in that mud alongside the road and just bury themselves and lay their eggs. It was fascinating. There was quite a few turtles.

**Ben Kern:**

BK June the 26th. We're laying over here at Chimney Rock. Going to lay over here today, and do some things and then we're gonna haul people, give wagon rides. And then we're gonna haul people up to the Michael Martin Murphey concert and then after it's over with, why, we're gonna give 'em a ride back down.

**Candy Moulton:**

CM The sun bore down on the wagons and the people at Chimney Rock. After endless days of rain, the sun finally came out in full force and the effect was harsh. People traveling with the train had blistered faces, and their hands were burned, cracked, and even bleeding from the constant exposure. Kris polished her harness as visitors asked questions about her team—questions that she'd answered hundreds of times in previous weeks. The sun beat down and she ignored the queries. Rudeness isn't natural, but perhaps understandable given the circumstances.

I wore a thin white cotton blouse and a blue calico skirt that came to the tops of my black, lace-up boots. I didn't pretend to be a pioneer, but opted for the skirt because it was much cooler than jeans when the mercury soared to the high nineties.

Camp sat a few hundred yards from the base of Chimney Rock and as I walked to the landmark, the tall buffalo grass caught on the hem of my skirt, pulling and tugging. The needle-sharp seed heads attached themselves to the material and soon formed a pincushion that tore at my bare legs above my boots. I pulled a few of the grass pieces from the cloth, but soon gave it up as hopeless. By nightfall, blood dotted my scratched legs.

As a crowd gathered for the concert, I visited backstage (behind the flatbed trailer) with Michael Martin Murphey, and kept an eye peeled for rattlesnakes. Murphey sang the ballads of

*Michael Martin Murphey sang cowboy ballads in a concert at the base of Chimney Rock to entertain residents and visitors to Western Nebraska in celebration of the 1993 wagon train.* (Candy Moulton Photo)

the old trail driving cowboys as the lights came on to illuminate Chimney Rock. But a full moon arcing across the sky, soon outshined the lights.

The emigrant diaries that described this rock vary in interpretation. Some say it was thirty feet high, others put it at two-hundred feet tall. Nebraska residents told me lightning hit it last summer and knocked a chunk off. I don't even know how to estimate the height—although some math teacher probably taught me the equation at one point—but I feel certain it's more than thirty feet from the base to the peak. Murphey sang his last ballad and began signing autographs, while I caught a ride down the mountain darkness in one of the wagons.

Hamilton Scott left Fremont, Iowa, April 24, 1862, headed for Walla Walla, Washington. He traveled with a large party including Thomas Paul, the Reverend Joseph Paul, Alvin Zaring and their families.

The travelers had three yoke of oxen and one yoke of cows to a team. On June 8 their train conducted a census which showed 220 people including 88 men, 46 women, and 86 children. They had 52 wagons, 315 head of cattle, and 38 mules.

Having a minister along on the trip gave the party an opportunity for worship services. On June 15, Scott wrote, "Had an exhortation from Father Paul at nine o'clock A.M." When the service ended the emigrants moved on toward the West.

Scott's diary chronicles their crossing of Western Nebraska:

HS ∩ June 16. Passed Chimney Rock. This rock stands on a sand bar and is thirty feet high and about six feet in diameter at the top. Saw some Indians today the first for about three hundred miles. Drove twenty miles today.

HS ∩ June 17. Tim Bailey's wife brought a new comer into camp last night which caused us to lay by today.

HS ∩ June 18. Passed Scott's Bluffs. Drove twenty-five miles and camped on the river near timber, the first for about two hundred miles. We have been using weeds and buffalo chips for fuel which answered very well on these desert plains.

HS ∩ June 20. Had a wedding in camp last night at nine o'clock. A couple from another train came in and had Rev. Joseph Paul tie the knot. We had an alarm in camp about eleven o'clock last night. The guards called three times, "Who comes there?" This was followed by about twenty shots in quick succession, at the same time "Indians! Indians! Indians! Help! Help!" was shouted. The camp was in great confusion, women were greatly alarmed. It turned out to be a white man trying to steal a horse and no Indians to be found. We drove 18 miles today.

Alvin Zaring, who traveled with Scott, added detail about the incident on June 20. He wrote:

AZ ∩ This mention of this Indian scare was written before the true nature of the circumstances were made known. Captain Kennedy thought best as we were [soon to] get out among the Indians, to test the bravery of the men in the train. He fell upon the plan to have the guards raise an alarm that the Indians were coming and attacking the horse guards. This caused quite an excitement. One old fellow jumped out of his wagon and getting on his knees, called upon the Lord for protection at the very top of his voice. Judging from the old fellow's daily life, I would think it was probably the first time he ever prayed.

**Ben Kern:**

BK June 27. We're leaving Chimney Rock and we're going to Gering and we're gonna camp at the Robidoux campground.

BK June 28. We left the Robidoux campground at 7:30 this morning and pulled up to the Scotts Bluff Monument. Went in there and circled the wagons, went through the monument and stayed there about an hour and left and we're now going toward Mitchell and we stopped here at a rancher's place and we're going to have dinner here.

[Later] we're in here at Mitchell at the rodeo grounds, and will make camp. Got a real nice camp site here, lots of grass and it looks like it's gonna be a good place to spend the afternoon and the evening.

SCOTTS BLUFF IS NAMED for Hiram Scott, an employee of General William H. Ashley's Rocky Mountain Fur Company who died there. Scott's Bluff was a major landmark for Oregon travelers who knew the plains were about to end and the mountains begin. They regrouped and prepared for the next big step on the way west. There in western Nebraska those who had their fill of trail travel turned back saying, "I saw the elephant."

BEN KERN:

BK June 29. We had a real bad rainstorm last night, hailed real bad, lots of thunder and lightning. We left Mitchell at 7:30 this morning. We're headed for Henry camp, this is going to be our last day in Nebraska.

[Later] we got in here to Henry camp about 4:30 and we're going to camp here tonight. The Governor of Nebraska and the Governor of Wyoming had a real nice ceremony last night. We all got certificates from the Nebraska tourism board, had a real nice supper.

A COUPLE OF CAMP COOKS came and went as the train crossed Nebraska. They cooked for a while then departed when they found conditions not to their liking. The necessity of feeding a family hasn't changed much in one hundred and fifty years. An 1857 traveler wrote that the choices of what to cook were limited, but that the physical labor required in preparing a meal seemed unlimited. Travelers gathered buffalo chips on the prairie to fuel a fire, then they squatted around it to prepare their meal, which often included only bread and bacon.

"One does like a change and about the only change we have from bread and bacon is to bacon and bread," Helen Carpenter wrote in 1857.

To make trail bread, women of the trains mixed soda and warm water, then added flour and salt to make a firm dough.

Sometimes they kneaded the dough while riding on the hard seat of a wagon. They cooked the bread by frying it in a skillet or putting it in a dutch oven. But trail cooking conditions weren't the best. If the women didn't have time to build a proper fire and wait for coals to form, the bread was likely to be burned on the outside and remain dough in the middle.

One admonition related to general conditions on the trail: "If mosquitoes are thick, they can get into the dough and turn it black. There is nothing you can do about this."

BEN KERN:

BK June 30. We're going to leave the Henry Camp here about 8:30 this morning. We're gonna cross the North Platte River and go back to the south side. The Wyoming governor, Mike Sullivan, is with us and we're gonna go over to the monument there on the line and we're gonna have a dedication. The governor helped me hitch up this morning and rode with me. He drove part of the time and we went south across the river and went out to the monument on the Wyoming-Nebraska border and we had a dedication with Mike Sullivan and then he departed.

We're headed right up the river toward Torrington. Keith Perry is taking us through this part of the trail, real pretty trail, lots of trees. One area here he said that when the wagon trains were going through a lot of people died with cholera. We stopped at a ranch and had dinner. The buildings are up on the hill and you can see a long ways, it's really a good place to stop, the owners have water tanks for the livestock. Lots of water.

We got into Torrington about three o'clock. People lined the streets and we really had a good reception. We got in and they fed us supper and they had the cowboy poets, real good deal. Kathy Karpan, Wyoming Secretary of State, rode with me this afternoon, she rode into Torrington. Waddie Mitchell and Don Edwards put on the cowboy poets deal and it was a really good show.

BK July 1. We're leaving the fair ground here at Torrington about 8:30 and we're going to Lingle and we're going to camp overnight there on a ranch. We had a real good runaway today, a team run off and went out across the ditch and went out through and broke a wheel so they're down, and can't travel. The runaway team belonged to some people traveling with us. We got into the ranch about 2:30–3 o'clock yesterday afternoon.

The Lingle community had a cream can feed last night, which was really good. They had about 350 people out here. They put potatoes, onions, corn, and carrots, along with meat, Polish sausage, into a cream can with a quart or so of water and then placed it in the fire and allowed it to cook for a few hours. To serve the dish, the cream can was emptied into a wash tub, and people helped themselves to a little of each item.

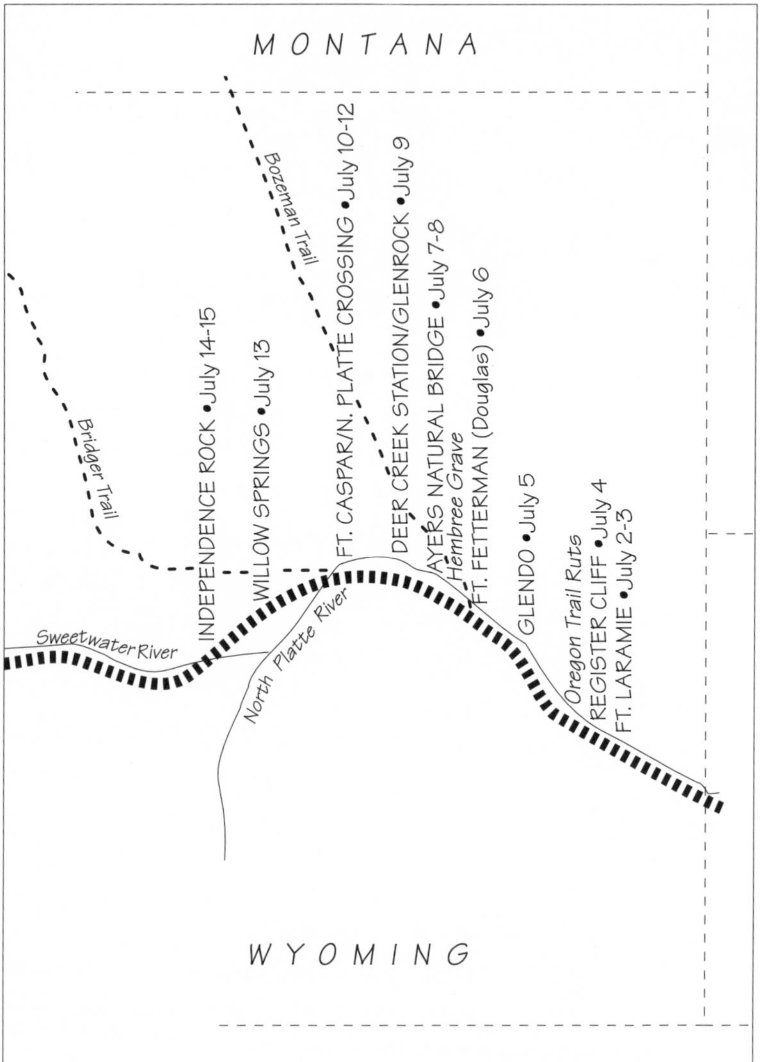

MONTANA

Bozeman Trail
Bridger Trail
INDEPENDENCE ROCK •July 14-15
WILLOW SPRINGS •July 13
FT. CASPAR/N. PLATTE CROSSING •July 10-12
DEER CREEK STATION/GLENROCK •July 9
AYERS NATURAL BRIDGE •July 7-8
Hembree Grave
FT. FETTERMAN (Douglas) •July 6
GLENDO •July 5
Oregon Trail Ruts
REGISTER CLIFF •July 4
FT. LARAMIE •July 2-3
Sweetwater River
North Platte River

WYOMING

**FORT LARAMIE TO INDEPENDENCE ROCK**

Progression of the 1993 Sesquicentennial Wagon Train

PART FOUR:

# Fort Laramie to Independence Rock

*Wherever we are, we're halfway between pretty soon and awhile ago.*
—Ben Kern, July 13, 1993

Fort Laramie, Wyoming. By the 1820s trappers gathered near where the Laramie River dumps into the North Platte, to rendezvous and trade goods. Among the early trappers was Jacques La Ramee, whose name is now associated with the fort and the river.

Robert Campbell and William Sublette had established a trading post on the banks of the Platte, called Fort William by 1834. In 1835 they sold the post to the American Fur Company. Not long after, the site became known as Fort John named for John B. Sarpy. A few years later it became Fort Laramie, when a clerk incorrectly wrote that address.

In 1842 John C. Frémont, who was exploring in the West, recommended that the fort become a military post to protect emigrants in their migration west. Seven years later the U.S. Government purchased Fort Laramie for $4,000 from the American Fur Company. The military retained the name Fort Laramie.

Ben Kern:

BK This is July the 2nd. We're gonna pull out of here

about 8:30 and we're gonna go to Fort Laramie today. Looks like it's gonna be a real pretty day. We're gonna go up the south side of the river.

We just went by the Grattan Monument. This was the spot where the Sioux Indians killed a calvary unit, they put up a monument here. We just came down the original ruts of the trail, we're headed into Fort Laramie. We can now see Laramie Peak in the distance. We got into Fort Laramie at 3 o'clock. There was sure a lot of people here to see us come in. We made a circle. We got a nice campsite here. They let us camp on the parade ground behind the bunkhouse and that was the first time a wagon train camped there since the early days, since the pioneer days.

BK July 3. We laid over all day, done repairs. Buck and I grazed the horses down along the river, done some repairs on the harness, made some new halter ropes, just done a few things in general. The wind really blowed. Blowed all day long, we had some 80 mile an hour winds, really a bad day. There weren't too many people out.

FROM ITS EARLIEST days, trappers, traders, and Indians gathered at Fort Laramie. An estimated ten thousand Sioux, Cheyenne, and Arapaho participated in the gathering that led to the Treaty of 1851, in which the tribes agreed to let wagon trains cross their lands in return for annual payments of goods valued at $50,000. Although their original gathering spot was near Fort Laramie, the tribes and the military officials later negotiated the treaty at Horse Creek, near the Wyoming-Nebraska border.

Many believe that treaty led to hostilities on the northern plains in subsequent years because the military leaders failed to live up to their promises. One of the first incidents that strained relations between the encroaching whites and the Indians after the treaty of 1851 occurred on August 19, 1854, just east of Fort Laramie.

Second Lieutenant John L. Grattan with twenty-nine soldiers, an interpreter, and a cannon, attempted to arrest a Miniconjou Sioux who had killed a cow that strayed from a Mormon emigrant, or perhaps was left behind when it became footsore. Grattan and his party entered the camp of the Brulé Sioux where the Miniconjou was staying.

The Indian wouldn't surrender. Grattan insisted and in the ensuing fight all but one member of the arresting party died. One enlisted man escaped and reached Fort Laramie, only to die later of his wounds. The soldiers shot Brulé Chief Brave Bear, who subsequently died in northeastern Nebraska.

Historians agree the incident was a misunderstanding. Nevertheless, it spurred hostilities along the Oregon Trail for the next several years including the previously related Bloody Blue fight the following year at Ash Hollow.

In 1850 William Riley Franklin headed from Missouri to California. Saturday, May 18, at Fort Laramie he wrote: "This looks like novelty to see the stars and stripes and serpent eagle, proudly wavering among the wild mountain breezes, [700] or 800 miles from the land whose representative it is, an among so many 1000 wild indians."

Emigrants saw Fort Laramie as a major point in their journey. It also marked one place where they crossed the North Platte River. June 11, 1859, Joseph Price wrote, "When we crossed the Platt down at Fort cearny we under Stood that we was clear of the Platt but the further we came up the more we became convinced that we was under a great mistake it is said that a mountain goat cant go up this side of the river and consequently we had to cross at this point."

For the most part travelers ferried across the river. By 1849 a privately-operated ferry served travelers. Later the army provided a ferry. The craft was a barge that remained in place until the army built a steel bridge in 1876, which still stands.

Once at Fort Laramie the travelers repaired wagons, bought whatever needed supplies they could and kept their faces pointed westward. Or, having seen the elephant, they exchanged the plains and mountains for the prairie and turned back.

Heinrich Lienhard in 1846 described Fort Laramie as "a rectangle with 16 to 20 foot walls of dried brick. The interior was divided into various rooms."

That same year Francis Parkman wrote: "Found ourselves before the gateway of Fort Laramie, under the impending blockhouse erected above it to guard the entrance.... The little fort is built of bricks dried in the sun, and externally is of an oblong form, with bastions of clay, in the form of ordinary blockhouses, at two of the corners."

There are bumps and humps, hollows and depressions that show where the early-day Fort Laramie buildings once stood. Many of the structures remain, either in the form of decaying stone foundations and walls or as renovated forms. Trees provide shade and boardwalks cover the footpaths. Now the National Park Service maintains the fort. Over along the river, a foot trail leads down the slope to a re-enactment trapper camp.

At the top of the slope, Fort William stood forth during the era of the mountain man. All that remains is an indentation in the soil filled with tall grass and prickly pear, blooming yellow in the summer sunshine.

Near the Fort Laramie visitors' parking lot, the Sutler's store, with its thick adobe walls, provides cool relief and cider or lemonade. It is certainly one of the oldest buildings remaining in Wyoming.

BEN KERN:

BK July 4. We left Fort Laramie at noon, there was sure lots of people out. The whole fort was full of people. We're headed for Guernsey. We're gonna stay at the Register Rock tonight on a ranch.

[Later] have a real nice spot here to camp, and the landowners furnished some hay, give us some water.

TWO WELL-KNOWN POINTS on the trail west of Fort Laramie are Register Cliff and the trail ruts, both near Guernsey. The meadow at the foot of Register Cliff, originally called Sand Point, served emigrants as the first stopping place west of Fort Laramie. Traders Seth Ward and William Guerrier kept a trading post at Register Cliff starting in 1841. Guerrier died in 1856 when a keg of powder in his wagon exploded. A man named Ecoffey, a close friend of Sioux Chief Red Cloud, operated a trading station at Register Cliff after 1854.

Register Cliff gets its title because emigrants carved their names in the soft sandstone wall. The names remain on the face of the cliff, many as clear as when they first appeared. Others are worn and somewhat illegible. Names and early dates mix with those of later-day visitors. One of the men traveling with Ben crossed a fence protecting the cliff section bearing the oldest names. High up on the sandstone cliff he carved his name in 1993, in large letters perhaps six inches tall.

Some people said he vandalized a historical landmark; others believe he had a right to carve his name because he crossed the trail with horses and wagons. It's there and it's new. The edges of the letters are sharp and light colored, unlike the older carvings, which have softened and faded under the winds of time.

The most remarkable set of Oregon Trail ruts on the entire two thousand mile route cut through solid sandstone near

Guernsey. The trail passed over the rocky hillside because the lower ground around the base was a slough. Wagon wheels ground the sandstone, creating the signature ruts.

Although the initial erosion took place as the result of Oregon migration, heavy freight wagons hauling material to Fort Laramie probably caused much of the wear. Freighters hauled material from a limestone quarry west of the ruts to Fort Laramie during its construction.

CANDY MOULTON:

CM I stood in the trace of the wagon wheels and wondered how the travelers kept their wagons from becoming high-centered or hung-up on the rocks. The sandstone warmed the land as it soaked the sun. When I sat at the peak of the crossing and rubbed my hand upon the stone, it became easy to imagine myself transported back in time.

A meadowlark trilled his sweet clear song and the wind rippled through the pines that cling to the rocky hillside. The echoes mixed with the echoes in my mind of men urging their animals over the sandstone. The wagon wheels ground the surface, gradually chipping away and forming a flaky powder in the trace.

I imagined women trudging beside and behind, holding their torn and tattered dresses up, away from the sharp rocks and the grasses and brush. I visualized the children, their energy unbounded by hundreds of miles, darting between the wagons and behind the trees.

The volume of traffic over the Oregon-California road in 1850 was staggering. Two letters written June 26 and July 7, 1850, quote figures from the log at Fort Laramie. In those eleven days, 933 wagons, 6,904 oxen, 544 mules, 1,465 horses, 1,988 cows, 2,817 men, 242 women, and 393 children registered as passing through Fort Laramie. And it's likely not everyone registered, so even more people and animals may have been on the trail during that brief span of time. The trail was literally a major thoroughfare with the people and animals stirring great clouds of dust as they headed west. All that traffic clearly points out, at least in 1850, the journey to Oregon or California was no lonely trip. Furthermore seeing an average of ninety wagons a day crossing any given point on the trail had to make a clear and sobering impression on the Native Americans. It certainly affected the wildlife, which scattered away from the trail, and had a profound impact on the range as all those grazing animals grubbed the land of most vegetation.

This place gave me my first sense of the trail as it was during the Great Migration since the train left Ash Hollow and Chimney Rock.

Wyoming will offer much more of the same as the wagons roll ever westward. Not much of the twenty-one hundred mile trail remains unscathed. Much of it is plowed and planted into corn and wheat and other crops. Entire sections lie beneath railroad beds and highway pavement. Ninety percent of the trail that remains basically unaltered is in Wyoming. Even more remarkable is the fact that sixty percent of the trail in Wyoming is on public land: ground that nobody wanted so it still belongs to the federal government and therefore, to all of us.

The wonderful result of that statistic is that anyone can see the trail. Any person can walk it, ride a horse over it, and in some areas drive on it. Few of the trail sections are pristine. Most show some recent use. For Rut Nuts—those people who love the trails and what they symbolize—the place to appreciate them is where they remain: on the high plains, mountain passes, and western deserts of Wyoming.

**Ben Kern:**

BK July 5. We left Register Rock and came right up along the North Platte River and we're on the old original ruts. We're south of Guernsey on the old original ruts and we're going to Glendo today. Now we're up on the divide here above Guernsey Dam. We got a good view of the dam and we got a good view of Laramie Peak.

[Later] we had lunch on Cottonwood Creek today and Keith Perry and his outfit, they just tied up and stayed there and we came on into Glendo. Never got into Glendo until about 8 o'clock, really a long day, but they put us up out here at the airport. Good place to camp. We really had a long day today. We done about 33 miles, but the horses handled it real good. My cousin, Howard Burton, came out. He owns a truck stop, store, and motel here and gave us four motel rooms to use and brought out some donuts.

A couple of miles west of Guernsey the wagons passed a warm spring known as the Emigrant's Laundry Tub because many did their washing in it. Virgil Pringle wrote June 24, 1846: "The spring is very bold and rather warm." Mormon Apostle Orson Pratt wrote June 5, 1847: "The name is Warm Spring; the water is not so cold as one would expect. The quantity is nearly sufficient to carry a common flour mill." William Clayton wrote in 1848: "This is a very strong spring of clear water, but it is warmer than river water, at all seasons of the year."

In 1854 Edwin Bird wrote of eastern Wyoming:

EB 1854 [Saturday June 10th]. This morning it was clear but clouded up before noon We have been going up & down all day long Saw Dogs harnessed up & used in packing This afternoon it rained in plain sight but we escaped. This eavning it is clear &

*Signature ruts near Guernsey, Wyoming.* (Candy Moulton Photo)

cold Have seen One old Grave To Knight we are camped upon the north fork of the Platt The senary has been important

EB ∩ Sunday 11th. Today there has been sun shine & shade In the afternoon it was showery off in the west where Laramas Peak rears its snow capt Sumit far above the surrounding mountains. The sumit of this mountain is covered with perpetual snow & can be see for a great distance We could see treas & kanyons upon it very plain it look to be about ten miles off But Mr Parks says it is forty five miles distant he says he has known men to start to visit it but after traveling over a rough road for one day have give it up saying it looked as far off at the end of their days journey as it did when they started Frémont says that it can be plainly see from Scotts Bluff upon a clear day I noticed several other peaks the names of which I did not learn We have now arived to where the black hills asume a rougher & lofter form here in realaty commences the Rockey Mountains that extensive range which nearly devides North Amercan We have wood & watter in abundance & nice spring watter at that therefore our campfires are plesant

Conditions on the Oregon Trail today are very different than what they were when the Great Migration of 1843 took place, but one thing that hasn't changed is the weather. Although modern travelers can follow highways, cross bridges, haul feed and fresh water, they can't control the elements.

In Kansas and eastern Nebraska both pioneers and modern-day travelers shivered in the cold and soaking rains. In western Nebraska and eastern Wyoming they watched tornadoes swirl by and they sweated under a burning sun. But the view has changed. Now near Douglas, Wyoming, oil pump jacks and power lines mar the land of its pristine emptiness.

Most often the writings of William Riley Franklin as he headed toward the gold fields of California in 1850 were filled with descriptions of the landscape through which his train was passing. But his journal also referred often to the people native to the land:

WRF ∩ Camp 29, Monday 20. In traveling up Platte River, the emigrants are astonished at the mornings, evenings and nights being so cold. This can be very easily accounted for. It is caused by the elevation and snow-clad mountains all around. I have been informed by the mountaineers that you can have ice water all the route, very near, by hanging out tin buckets with water in them during the night. Who can comprehend the wisdom of God. How wisely has he made provisions for those who by circumstances or by his infinite wisdom been scattered over the earth's wide domain by forming those eternal snow-clad rocky mountains which is an everlasting haven to their enemies and a sure refuge from their preservers. The provisions nature has also filled those same mountains with game of all kinds and varieties for their sustenance. Notwithstanding all this, there is something in the poor Indians' fate that awakens the sympathy of every philanthropic nation and individual, especially the christian. There is something about their origin, manners and etc., that never will be fairly understood.... Their history seems to be a sealed book which none of the sons of men can open.

BEN KERN:

BK July 6. We're leaving Glendo this morning, headed for Douglas. We're at Orin Junction and we're going to water horses and have dinner. We got into Douglas at the fairgrounds about 5:30 and we camped down here in the fairgrounds.

BK July 7. We're gonna leave for Natural Bridge this morning. We're getting a late start. It's about 8:30 now and we're gonna go out on a ranch and camp there tonight.

I am up on the hill just above our camp at the gravesite of Joel Hembree. A marker says: Joel Jordan Hembree, his wife Sara, and their eight sons from McMinnville, Tennessee, were a part of the estimated 1,000 men, women and children who left Fitzhugh's mill near Independence, Missouri, in May 1843 for Oregon. On July 18, between Bed Tick Creek and here at LaPrele Creek six-year-old Joel Hembree, the second youngest son, fell from the wagon tongue on which he was riding and was fatally injured.

Diarist William T. Newby wrote July 18th: "A very bad road. Joel J. Hembrees son Joel fell off the waggeon tongue."

THE FIRST CASUALTY in the "Great Migration" of 1843 was six-year-old Joel Hembree, who died after falling under a wagon, which passed over his body. Apparently injured on July 18, 1843, the boy died the following day and was buried on LaPrele Creek west of Douglas on July 20, his body protected by an old oak dresser drawer.

July 20, 1843, James W. Nesmith wrote, "at noon came up to a fresh grave with stones piled over it, and a note tied on a stick, informing us that it was the grave of Joel J. Hembree, aged six years, who was killed by a wagon running over its body. At the head of the grave stood a stone containing the name of the child, the first death on the expedition. The grave is on the left hand side of the trail close to Squaw Butte Creek."

A later traveler, Matthew C. Field, wrote of finding the pile of stones marking the boy's grave. "How he died we cannot of course surmise, but there he sleeps among the rocks of the West, as soundly as though chiseled marble was built above his bones."

Traveler Edwin Bird wrote in 1854:

EB ∩ Monday [June] 12th. This morning it was clear but about noon there came up a thunder storm but it passed around us we were all wishing that it might rain it however layed the dust ahead of us.... Came through one place which looks as though it had been on fire. The whol ground sounded like a drum as we passed over it. Saw any quantaty of red clay or earth in other places there is large quantaties of plaster.... The first stream of any importance was Labonta it is clear & very cold & swift & runs down from the mountains To knight we are camped on the banks of the Laprell or Rusk Crick like the most of the streams the onley treas that shades its banks are cotton & willow.

IN THE AREA BETWEEN Douglas and Glenrock pioneer routes known as the Fetterman Trail and the Bozeman Trail headed to the north, into Powder River Country.

John Jacobs and John Bozeman pioneered the trail—following known Indian routes—that carries the latter's name, opening it in 1864 as a shorter route to Montana's gold fields. But the land the route crossed belonged to the Sioux under the treaty of 1851. The Indians fought their hardest battles of the Plains Indian Wars to retain the Powder River Basin as their territory.

Among the confrontations between the Sioux and the U.S. Army was a fight north of Fort Phil Kearny on December 21, 1866. Lieutenant William J. Fetterman and eighty-one men pursued Sioux over Lodgepole Ridge. When the dust settled, Fetterman and all of his men lay dead along the route of the Bozeman Trail. It was one of many violent fights between the Indians and military, and the Bozeman Trail became known as the Bloody Bozeman.

Lakota leader Red Cloud demanded that the whites abandon the Bozeman Road and in 1868 the military agreed. They left the area, and the Sioux immediately burned three forts: C.F. Smith in southern Montana Territory, and Phil Kearny and Reno in Wyoming Territory.

In the summer of 1867, the military had started construction of a fort located northwest of Douglas named Fort Fetterman, for Lieutenant William J. Fetterman. After 1876 and the battle at Little Big Horn between Crazy Horse, Sitting Bull, and Lieutenant George A. Custer, another route into the Powder River country opened for use as a freighting route between Rock Creek Station in southern Wyoming Territory on the Union Pacific Railroad line and Montana Territory. It became known as the Fetterman Trail.

*Casper Star-Tribune* reporter Deirdre Stoelzle wrote July 9, 1993, as she rode with the wagons:

DS You know when you're at the crossing of the Fort Fetterman and Oregon trails by the yellow sweet clover X over the plains.

We're told that those traveling west and north during the Great Migration planted the sweet clover seed for their successors on the trails, for feed. At the crossing those on the wagon train wait while video cameras and one-touch, modern miracle cameras are taken with some riders to the top of the hill. It takes ten minutes, maybe longer, for everyone to pose for panoramic views, close up views, and other shots....

Sage is heavy in the air and there's only hills and plains for miles before civilization takes the forms of the Dave Johnston Power Plant, plenty of power poles and wires, and then of course Interstate 25, along which we traveled.

Everyone is sunburned.

Probably the best thing to do while you're traveling westward on the Trail is to fall in love. It definitely would lessen the boredom of riding, riding, riding, and bumping, bumping, bumping over the ruts and down the slopes.

BEN KERN:

BK July 8. We traveled to Natural Bridge and camped at the Joel Hembree gravesite. The landowner had a big flatbed trailer and was scattering sprinkler pipe to irrigate fields.

A COUPLE OF MILES farther west of the Hembree grave is the beautiful red rock Ayres Natural Bridge across La Prele Creek. On July 12-14, 1843, Matthew C. Field wrote that his party went to visit the area. He described it thus:

MF 1843. ...a remarkable mountain gorge—a natural bridge of solid rock, over a rapid torrent, the arch being regular as tho shaped by art—30 feet from base to ceiling, and 50 to the top of the bridge—wild cliffs, 300 feet perpendicular beetled above us, and the noisy current swept along among huge fragments of rock at our feet. We had a dangerous descent, and forced our way through an almost impervious thicket, being compelled to take the bed of the stream in gaining a position below. We called the water "Bridge Creek!"

THE NATURAL BRIDGE arcs over the creek in an original amphitheater of red sandstone walls. Protected by the rocks, the area below the rock bridge is lush and green during summertime. The water ripples over the rocks and gravel in the stream, gurgling under the bridge. Birds soar on the thermals above the box canyon and heavy, old cottonwoods provide shade.

BEN KERN:

BK July 9. We left Natural Bridge, on the way to Glenrock. We stopped at a ranch for lunch and to feed our horses. Got into Glenrock at the park about 5 o'clock. There was lots of people here to meet us, to greet us. The town of Glenrock had a dedication for us when we got in. They also cooked us supper, had a big barbecue for us.

THE DAYS ON THE trail become an endurance test. Leeann fell asleep as she drove one day along a state highway. She always wore her black hat pulled real low over her eyes and on that particular day hunkered down on the seat and let her eyes become mere slits. Before long she dozed. Her team veered to the left, right into the path of an oncoming semi-truck, but Maggie and Molly turned back into the line of the wagons on their own and the truck passed harmlessly.

Mountain men guided John C. Frémont when he headed west to map the country for later travelers. On July 26, 1842, he

*Ayres Natural Bridge crosses La Prele Creek in east-central Wyoming, a "natural bridge of solid rock," as Mathew C. Field described it in 1843.* (Candy Moulton Photo)

wrote, "reached the mouth of Deer Creek, where we encamped ... abundance of rich grass ... [stream] twenty feet broad, and well timbered with cottonwood of an uncommon size."

The trail ran south of the North Platte. Indian trader Joseph Bissonette established a trading complex that included a store, blacksmith shop, and post office. Indians had a ford across the North Platte at the mouth of Deer Creek, and Bissonette established a ferry of six or eight dugout canoes across the river about a half mile upstream. He operated the ferry in 1849 and 1850, mainly to serve the gold rush traffic. The ferry may have been propelled with oars or pulled with a line.

At Deer Creek July 16, 1849, J. Goldsborough Bruff wrote of the crossing ..."passing through hundreds of tents, wagons, camp fires, and people of every age & sex, congregated on its banks, and turned down to the right, camped on the banks of Platte, at the Ferry."

Glenrock is the site of an old campground known as the Rock in the Glen, where thousands of emigrants camped on their way west. The area was a Mormon way station by 1850, but the Mormons abandoned it during the Mormon War of 1857. Then "Major" Thomas Twiss, Indian agent at Fort Laramie, promptly packed up his agency and moved it a hundred miles up the Platte to the abandoned station. He took up residence in the Mormon houses with his Oglala bride and his pet bear.

From his new station, which he called the Upper Platte River Agency, Twiss administered his Indian affairs until President Abraham Lincoln removed him in 1861. That same year the military established Deer Creek Station just south of the Oregon Trail and slightly northwest of Glenrock.

Edwin Bird in 1854 wrote:

EB ∩ 1854. This fournoon the sky was overcast by thin hasy clouds about the maridinth of the day heavy black clouds sprung up in evry direction & this afternoon thunder storms have completely walled us in with there black frunts while the vivid lightnings are playing there firy pranks in evry direction We had fulley made up our minds to get a soking but the clouds broke & the storm passed around us onley sprinkling us a little We have been travling over a smooth roling road To knight we are camped on the Platt & close to Dear Crick which is a clear nice stream Near our camp is a large sand stone rock which I shall call Lone Cedar as there is a solatary & very prety cedar beded in the solid rock

In 1860 Sir Richard Burton on an excursion in the West wrote:

RB ∩ 1860. Deer Creek, a stream about thirty feet wide.... The station boasts an Indian agent, Major Twiss, a post office, a store, and of course a grog-shop. M. Bissonette, the owner of the two latter and an old Indian trader, was the usual creole, speaking a French not unlike that of the Channel Islands and wide awake to the advantages derivable from travellers.... I wish my enemy no more terrible fate than to drink excessively with M. Bissonette.

Our station lay near the upper crossing or second bridge, a short distance from the town. It was also built of timber at an expense of $40,000, about a year ago, by Louis Guenot, a Quebecquois, who has passed the last twelve years upon the plains. He appeared very downcast about his temporal prospects...the usual toll is $0.50, but from trains, especially Mormons, the owner will claim $5; in fact, as much as he can get without driving them to the opposition lower bridge [Richard], or to the ferry boat.

John Baptiste Richard, [pronounced and sometimes spelled Reshaw] built the first bridge across the Platte in 1851. It sat just upstream from Bissonette's ferry. Joined by other men, Richard also had a toll bridge across the river at Fort Laramie.

After a spring flood took out Richard's first bridge, he built another in 1852 at a site now in Evansville, not far from Ben Kern's house. It served as a toll bridge periodically until 1865, but wasn't profitable during later years because of another bridge—Old Platte Bridge—constructed by Louis Guinard in 1858.

BEN KERN:

BK July 10. We left Glenrock for Casper. We had a lot of people ride with us today. A lot of horseback riders, a lot of people riding in the wagons. And there were people all along the road. We followed the old highway. We stopped at Edness Kimball Wilkins Park for lunch. They had a big lunch for us and there were really a lot of people. We laid over a couple of hours at the park then we left and headed for Casper to our camp at Fort Caspar. There was lots and lots of people all along the roadway and lots of people all through Casper. We traveled on the old highway on the south side of the river. The streets of downtown Casper were packed with people.

IN 1847 MORMONS constructed and operated the first ferry across the North Platte at the site that eventually became Fort Caspar. It remained in use until 1851. Brigham Young selected nine men to operate the ferry, which was made of two large cottonwood canoes fastened together and covered with slabs.

The Mormon Ferry served two purposes: it provided safe passage across the North Platte and funds for new settlements in the Great Salt Lake valley.

At Upper Ferry William Riley Franklin wrote: "Today we traveled over the most dreary desolate sandy and parched country that we have yet seen. Scarcely any growth but the wild Sage which usurps the place of grass, and was subsequently our chief reliance for fuel. Here at the ferry the river is about, or will average, 150 yards wide and is a bold running stream."

Adobe buildings were erected near the Mormon Ferry in 1858 and in 1859 troops arrived to protect wagons along the Oregon Trail.

The military established Fort Caspar—originally known as Platte Bridge Station—in 1858 and abandoned it in 1859. But the military reactivated the station in 1862 to keep communications open and guard emigrants along the trail corridor. It remained garrisoned until 1867. It is named for Lieutenant Caspar Collins, but the fort and the town use different spellings, similar to Fort Kearny and Kearney, Nebraska.

Ben Kern:

BK July 11. We are laying over three days at Casper, at Fort Caspar. It is quite emotional to get this far. It is good to be home for a short period of time. I came home and washed clothes, and sorted a lot of my stuff and am leaving a lot of stuff behind that I think I won't need. I am leaving my long handled underwear at home.

I have had and will keep a lot of extra clothes. I figure I can go a couple or three weeks without washing them and still change my clothes if I get wet and damp. I have extra boots and extra shoes and extra hats. I have a couple of good hats along and I have 'em in a box, but I never get 'em out. I just wear the one same old hat all the time.

At Platte Bridge in 1854 Edwin Bird wrote:

EB 1854. This morning it was clear & cold Soon after sunrise it clouded up accompanyed by a strong west wind came about ten miles & crossed the north fork of the Platt here we found a good bridge far better than som I have seen at home There is a store & other buildings connected with it.... The owner of the bridge says that he took in seventeen thousand dollars last season he charges five dollars for a team & five cents a head for loos stock We join the Council Buluff Road here so we are all in a string & never out of sight of a train Here we leave the Platt which has become a small clear swift & cold stream & strike across to the Sweet Waughter To knight we are camped in the Crow Indian Teratory near a little stream that is tinctured with alchali.

BIRD'S REFERENCE to joining the Council Bluff road is an indication that the Oregon and Mormon Trails joined here. Across Nebraska and eastern Wyoming the Oregon route ran on the south bank of the Platte and the Mormons used a trail on the northern side.

The Oregon Trail west of Casper is the same route as the Mormon Trail. Although Mormons first moved west with wagons starting in 1847, their trek is most often referred to in terms of the handcart companies. Ten handcart companies involving 2,945 people went from Florence, Nebraska, to Salt Lake City between 1856 and 1860. Five companies traveled the first year, two in 1857, one in 1859, and two in 1860.

Most handcart pioneers made the journey under the Perpetual Emigration Fund. Although they provided some of their own money and resources for the trip, the church purchased by far the majority of their supplies. Although many Mormons came from the Midwest, as the years passed, a larger number of Saints came from England, Finland, and Ireland.

Mormon missionaries worked hard in those countries to spread the word of their religion and to recruit Saints to make the trip to America. Many of the people had little in those foreign lands, and they carefully saved what they could in order to emigrate. Stories are recorded of women hoarding money for years in order to help their families come to America and travel to the Mormon Zion. Most of those who came from England, Ireland, and the European countries did so under provisions of the Perpetual Emigration Fund provided by the church.

Some sailed to New York and then used rail transportation to Council Bluffs, Iowa. Others rode the ocean to New Orleans, then followed the Mississippi north to Nauvoo, Illinois, and then migrated to Council Bluffs. In nearly all cases, they had little food on the journey, and they faced much hardship before they even started the long trek across the prairie, plains, and mountains to Utah. Sometimes the trip became tragic.

Besides the joining of the Mormon and Oregon Trails at Casper, another short-lived pioneer trail has its genesis in central Wyoming. When John Jacobs and John Bozeman attempted to take gold seekers over their route through the Powder River Basin and into Montana, the Sioux raised all kinds of chaos.

The Indians demanded that the military and the white emigrants stay out of the Powder River country east of the Big Horn Mountains. In return, however, the Sioux agreed not to create problems for travelers following the Bridger Trail—a route which crossed along the west side of the Big Horns and passed out of Sioux territory.

Jim Bridger began trapping in the 1820s and knew the mountains, rivers, basins, and valleys of Wyoming as well as any man. In the Bloody Plains year of 1865 he pioneered a route to Montana taking off from Platte Bridge Station and heading west, then north across the Big Horn River and through the Big Horn Basin.

The route became a double-edged sword. The travelers had no problems with Indians, but they crossed a desert country of badlands with little water and scarce game. As a result the Bridger Trail saw only limited use.

BEN KERN:

BK July 13. We left Fort Caspar headed for Willow Springs. This was a morning of a lot of mixed emotions for me.

I have a lot of reservations about leaving here and going on, but I am determined to finish this regardless of what happens. I'm not going to quit here. I definitely want to finish what we started to do. Leaving home again and going on.... I have a lot of thoughts about it.

Today was really a rough day. It was a long one. A lot of mileage. We went out through Emigrant Gap and up Poison Spider Creek, through the Avenue of Rocks. We had a lot of people on the wagons. The wagons were pretty well loaded and we were pulling a lot of weight this day so the horses were working a lot harder today than they normally would. The wind was blowing real hard and when we started up Ryan Hill we unloaded a lot of people and had them walk up the hill and the wind was blowing so hard it ripped the top right off my wagon. The canvas acted like a balloon and I thought it was going to tip my wagon over.

This is a real bad camp. It is all sagebrush, real high sagebrush and we had to camp right in the sagebrush. We had a couple from Oregon that got married tonight as we were in camp.

As Ben's wagon pulled away from Fort Caspar, Claudette Ortiz, Letters Editor with the *Casper Star-Tribune* rode with him. She wrote the following for the July 14, 1993, issue of the paper:

CO One hundred and fifty years later, most of us don't know a stampede string from a dashboard, but then, Francis Parkman, who rode and wrote *The Oregon Trail* didn't know an Indian from an enthusiasm.

It's an enthusiasm to ride on this journey; to leave phone, fax and modem is something that doesn't compute. This is where the pavement ends and Emigrant Gap begins.

It is here in this isolated area that a herd of horses gallops over to get a closer look at the wagon train. An old doe looks up from

*The wide North Platte River just west of Casper, Wyoming.* (Candy Moulton Photo)

her babysitting chore with five baby antelope. A young buck, still in velvet with forked horn, leaps across Poison Spider Road.

Blackbirds bunch, the certain calligraphy of an early Fall. And a turtledove makes a confused detour through the wagon and out again....

Thoughts on a wagon are sunbaked by the prairie, cooled by the winds, and at four miles an hour, slow to rise. They kind of roll over on the tongue and go back to bed. Whatever it was, it'll keep. It's like the driver Ben Kern says, "Wherever we are, we're halfway between pretty soon and awhile ago."

BEN KERN:

BK July 14. It got cold last night. The temperature got down to about 20 degrees. We left Willow Springs for Independence Rock. This part of the trail is the old original trail. We crossed the highway and then went across the Pathfinder Ranch and that was called the alkali flats, or soda flats, and this is right along the old original trail to Independence Rock. We'd been watching Independence Rock and Devil's Gate since we left Willow Springs. We got to Independence Rock about 4 o'clock.

We're camped on the east side of Independence Rock. At Casper some other people joined us with their three teams and wagons. They each had a six horse hitch. Standard horses, they left camp after us, but because the standard horses move faster they caught up with us. They were right behind us when we pulled in to Independence Rock.

West of Fort Laramie the most noted landmark on the Oregon Trail is Independence Rock. Robert Stuart and his companions, returning from Fort Astoria in 1812, saw the rock before constructing the first known building in Wyoming at Bessemer Bend where they stayed for several days prior to continuing their eastern-bound journey.

Independence Rock is mostly likely named from the sojourn of mountain man Thomas Fitzpatrick and companions at its base on July 4, 1824, but some say it was christened by William L. Sublette and Moses Harris on July 4, 1831.

It certainly had the name by 1835 when Reverend Samuel Parker wrote: "Passed Rock Independence.... This is the first massive rock of that stupendous chain of mountains which divides North America and forms together with its barrens on either side a natural division. This rock takes its name from the circumstances of a company of fur traders suspending their journey and here observing in due form the anniversary of our national freedom."

In 1834, John K. Townsend mentioned in his diary that he camped at "a large rounded mass of granite, about fifty feet high, called Rock Independence." Father Pierre De Smet in 1840, referred to the "famous rock, Independence . . . that might be called the great registry of the desert, for on it may be read in large characters the names of several travelers who have visited the Rocky Mountains."

In 1842, John Charles Frémont described the rock:

JCF ∩ 1842. About 650 yards long and 40 in height. Except in a depression on the summit, where a little soil supported a scanty growth of shrubs with a solitary pine, it was entirely bare. Everywhere within six or eight feet from the ground, where the surface was sufficiently smooth, and in some place sixty or eighty feet above, the rock was inscribed with names of travelers. . . . I engraved on this rock of the far West a symbol of the Christian faith . . . a large cross, which I covered with a black preparation of India rubber well calculated to resist the influence of wind and rain.

In 1847 Brigham Young led the first group of Mormons past the spot and by 1855 some of Young's followers, who had stone cutting tools, conceived the idea of engraving travelers' names on the rock at a cost of $1 to $5 a name.

Lieutenant Caspar Collins, for whom Fort Caspar and the city of Casper are named, commanded the post at the crossing of the Sweetwater River near Independence Rock, for a time. Collins wrote to his mother in Ohio, June 16, 1862: "This is the worst country for winds I ever saw. Yesterday . . . it commenced to blow, and it is blowing yet. . . . Major Bridger went off this morning up in the mountains to get out of the wind. He says he is going to get in some canon and make a large fire."

None of the emigrants on the Oregon Trail relied on the land for their sustenance. Even so, often the men had an opportunity for sport and dietary variety as they hunted buffalo, antelope, wolves or rattlesnakes.

Edwin Bird wrote in 1854:

EB ∩ Wensday 14th [June]. To day resembles yesterday Traveled untill noon when we camped near the Platt.... Have had quite a time killing one of those large yellow Rattle Snakes which abound in the Rockeys he ran into his hole leaving nuthing but his tail to be see with which he played us a lively tune we made a slip knot in a whip lash shiped it down below his musical instrument which if I remember right numbered twenty drew him forth strait way & shot him with a revolver This afternoon we are laying over som are improving the time in writing Som are playing cards while quite a number have goan out a hunting The Hunters were luckey & brought into camp a fine Antalope we are all expecting a raraty now & no mistake & licking our chops in antisapation of to morrow... To knight for the first time we have wild sage for fuel this is a specia of wood which grows in bunches it varies in hight from one foot to 8 ft but the general avrage is about 2 feet it burns verey well onley that it does not last long

At Independence Rock in 1854 Hamilton Scott wrote:

HS ∩ Sunday 18th [June]....After coming two miles we passed Independence Rock this seems to be formed of gravel stones of diferent hues & very brilant semented by nature into a solid rock I think I am purfectly safe in saying that [it] is the greatest register in all the west, being covered with names bearing dates from 1836 to 1854 many of them are yet verey plain & some of them will stand for many years to come I should juge that the highest point of the rock is 90 feet In the distance it looks like a long hay stack, it is also ribed I think that the watter runing off of it for ages has wear these chanels & leaving the harder part of the rock in riges. But what is still more strange & what perhaps would mistify my argument above, is, that the riges are at regular intervals apart & run in strate lines over the rock We have crossed the Sweet Watter found a good brige & several Trading posts located here.

The Declaration of Independence and battles of the Revolutionary War had deep meaning to the generation that formed the nucleus of the Oregon migration. Their immediate ancestors fought the battles. The Americans who headed west to settle Oregon country were on the trail because they wanted land and better opportunities. Also, they wanted to lay firm claim to the region and once again force out the British.

For most emigrants, Independence Day not only reminded them of the freedoms so courageously won from the British, but it also served as an admonition that they should be at or near Independence Rock on July 4 if they expected to reach Oregon before snowfall closed the mountain passes in the fall.

The Forty-Niners heading toward California's gold fields traveled more swiftly than did families and often were at Bear River in Idaho by the Fourth of July. The Mormons with handcarts in the Willie and Martin companies of 1856 hadn't even left eastern Nebraska by July 4. Their delay in departing came to haunt them in October as they struggled across the snow-swept Sweetwater valley in Wyoming.

After the wearing monotony of trail travel, Independence Day also marked one rare moment for fun and frolic.

An 1853 wagon train celebration included a menu that had cake, pies, preserves, butter, rice, biscuits, sausage, tea and coffee along with a "fruit cake baked back home in Illinois and saved for the celebration."

*A view of circled wagons at Independence Rock, with Devil's Gate in the background, as painted by William Henry Jackson.* (Photo Courtesy of Scotts Bluff National Monument)

That same year Helen Stewart wrote: "... this is the fourth in the States a great many ... is prepareing for pleasure of some kind but we are selerabrating it by traviling in sand and dust but we had a great dance tonight.... I went up on the hill and talked over old times ... and then we come down and danced untill neerly one oclock it done very well for want of better fun it is a beautiful eavening the star shine bright we have excelent grass."

Emigrant Edwin Bird wrote Tuesday July 4, 1854:

EB ∩ 1854. This morning about one o'clock the gards commenced to welcom in the glorious fourth aday sacred to every American by discharging their revolvers which was soon answered from camp this was the onley way we could celabrate but we thought of the sturing times at home the Orations the boom of Canon, bands of martial music pleasure rides prety Girls & Ball Rooms. The imagination had to take the place of the realaty It has been a clear day with a good refreshing breas the atmosphere assumes a smoky apperance like Indian Sumer.

For some Independence Day was a time for celebration, but others saw little change in their traveling routine. Hamilton Scott's party reached Independence Rock on July 4 where he wrote:

HS ∩ Drove twelve miles, camped at noon, having to bury one of our company boys here. Bovee's death was accidental and was a very sad affair. While he and another man were hunting wolves in the bluffs about two miles from the train, Bovee shot one. The wolf fell down a crevice between the rocks. When Bovee stooped to scalp the animal, his revolver fell from the holster, hitting a rock and shooting him through the heart. He lived only a few minutes. He leaves a wife and two children. Poor woman, it will be hard for her.

Ben Kern:

BK July 15. We will lay over at Independence Rock two days. I climbed the rock. It makes you wonder, think about how that rock was ever put here. There was lots of people at Independence. They had a lot of people here. About three or four in the afternoon we had a bad windstorm. A lot of people got up and left on account of the storm.

I spent much of the day with Dennis Sun to check out the trail. He had a couple of different routes that we could go when we left from Independence Rock to Split Rock. As we were going down the trail checking out the trail, Dennis and I were driving along talking and we had our windows down and the road kind of went under a bank and there was a rattler there and he rattled at us. Dennis and I both at the same time said, "There's a rattlesnake." Dennis backed up and there he was up on the bank coiled up and Dennis said, "I guess we'll just leave him" and we went on. He was a big rattlesnake.

Dennis was pretty well supplied. We had a case of beer when we left and we were doing a lot of visiting and talking about the country and different things and different happenings and by the time we got to Split Rock at our camp there on Doc Baker's we were out of beer so Dennis decided maybe we better go to Jeffrey City and get some more beer so we went on to Jeffrey City and had a couple of beers in the bar and we bought a case of beer and then Dennis wanted to kind of show me some more of their ranch holdings and whatnot.

At that time they were catching wild horses. So we went to the U. S. Bureau of Land Management wild horse trap where they were catching horses. On the way to Green Mountain we saw a barn at the ranch that was painted in 1922 with Rawlins Red paint. To look at it it looked like it was just painted yesterday or the day before. It was still in great shape. We stopped at this other ranch and visited a while then we went on.

We went to Muddy Gap and we were out of beer again so we stopped and bought some more. Then we returned back to Independence Rock. Had a real good day. I enjoyed visiting with Dennis. He's a good person. He related a lot of history to me today about their ranch and the Oregon Trail.

CANDY MOULTON:

CM Leeann turned sixteen July 15 with a day-long birthday celebration on the east side of Independence Rock. Accompanied by family members, I drove three hours to join the wagons for a party at Independence Rock. The event, staged by Carbon County residents, drew hundreds of people who scrambled like ants over the turtle-shaped granite outcropping.

Lichen covered the granite and hardy wildflowers bloomed in cracks and crevices. Climbing Independence Rock surprised me by its ease. I'd never been to the top and expected a slicker

*Candy Moulton sitting on top of Independence Rock, with the Sweetwater River in the background.* (Penny Walters Photo)

surface. I watched Elmer Armstrong, an old man who's had brain surgery, totter to the top of the rock and figured if he could climb it I could as well. His wife stood at the base of the granite and worried for his safety. "He shouldn't be doing that," Alma told me. Elmer participated in a Boy Scout Jamboree here as a youngster and he had climbed the rock then. Now it had become a challenge to do so again. I told Alma he wanted to make the climb. She fretted and reluctantly agreed. Later I saw the two of them listening to the music. He had an ear-to-ear grin; she hovered like a protective hen.

My mother, my sister, and my children accompanied me on my own jaunt up the rock. From the rock's crown the view was pure Wyoming—a wide view of sagebrush and native grasses, broken occasionally by rocky outcroppings and small ponds of water. The snaky Sweetwater ribboned through the valley, but it has a new channel. That was clear from the horseshoe shaped areas where the stream doesn't run any more. As I sat atop the rock, the blue water looked inviting and must have been because I saw three young boys splashing with their dog.

I saw Oregon Trail ruts leading into and away from the rock. White stakes marked the route on the south side and the deep swale extended east of Wyoming Highway 220. Most emigrant trains stopped here and almost every journal and diary I've read mentions the place.

It's said that during the peak years of migration wagons were a steady line between here and Fort Laramie. Emigrants carved their names all over this rock, and I traced my finger on some of their etchings.

The celebration for the wagon train included music—cowboy, jazz, and trail songs—played on instruments ranging from trumpets and guitars to pan lids and even a plastic bird.

The emigrants often celebrated when they got here—perhaps with music from a harmonica or fiddle. They knew they'd spend days following the Sweetwater, and they had 815 miles of the 2,000 mile journey behind their worn wagon wheels.

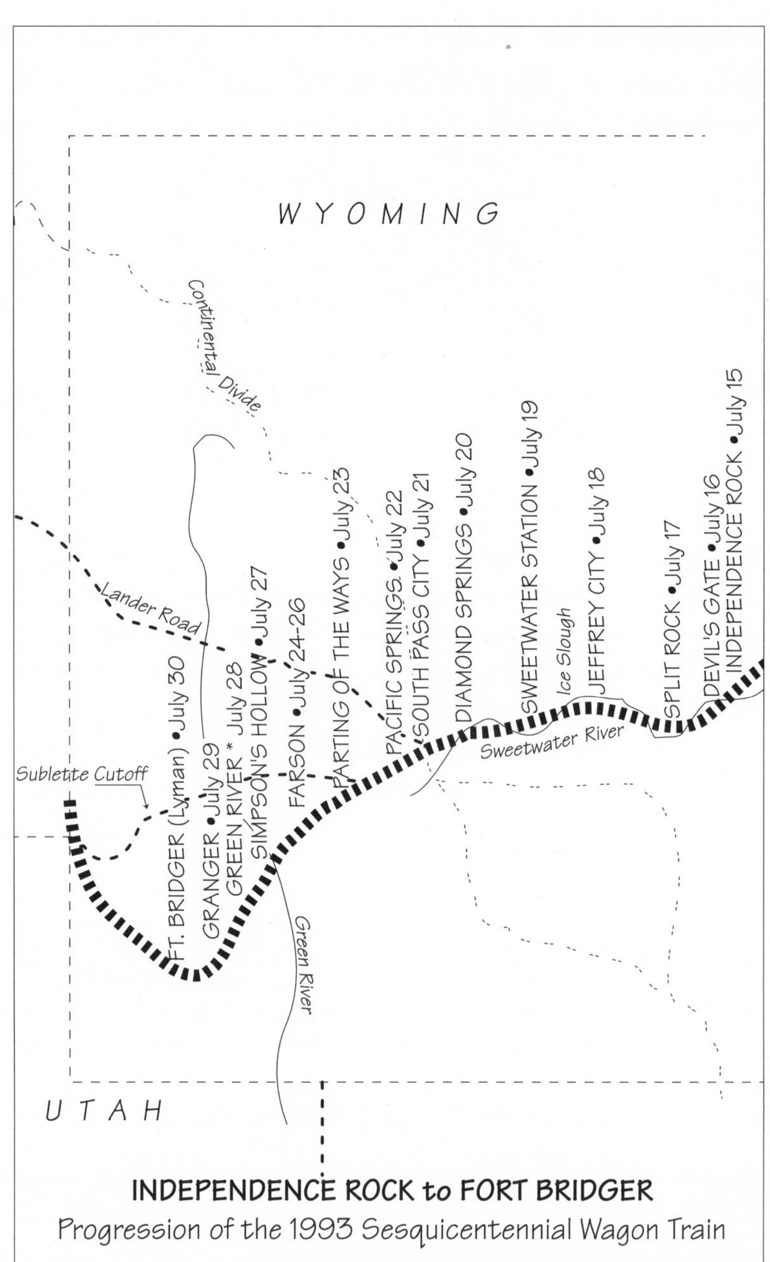


**INDEPENDENCE ROCK to FORT BRIDGER**

Progression of the 1993 Sesquicentennial Wagon Train

PART FIVE:

# Independence Rock to Fort Bridger

*"They talk about the times that tried men souls but if thes ware not the times that tried both men and wemon's souls."*
—Elizabeth Stewart Warner, in 1853

Devil's Gate, Wyoming. The Sweetwater River flows through a narrow break in the towering rocks west of Independence Rock at a place called Devil's Gate. Some say it is a gloomy place and could be violent when the water raced through in flood stage, so the place earned its satanic appellation.

In 1840 Pierre De Smet passed the area without mentioning the site, but in a letter dated August 16, 1841, he said "travelers have named this spot the Devil's Entrance." In 1843 journalist Matthew C. Field called it "Hell Gate."

Ben Kern:

BK July 16. We left Independence Rock and came to Devil's Gate. Tonight we were setting up camp and the people from KTWO television came to interview me for a piece to run on Labor Day for Jerry's Kids and MD. We really had a problem getting the tipis up. The wind is blowing. Couldn't keep the tipis up, in fact we never did get them all up. The people will sleep in the wagons or wherever they can find. It is really cold again tonight. The wind is blowing.

*Wagons pass near Devil's Gate in this painting by William Henry Jackson.* (Photo Courtesy of Scotts Bluff National Monument)

BK July 17. We left camp this morning, left Devil's Gate. We went to the Sun Ranch and then we forded the river there at the ranch. Then we went down to Devil's Gate and we circled the wagons and took pictures with Devil's Gate in the background. While we were crossing the river there at the Sun Ranch one of the wagons that had joined us got stuck in the river and Shawn and I unhooked one of the teams. Shawn was driving and I was holding the double trees and we waded in the river and then we had to take a chain. We hooked onto the end of the tongue and around the double trees and we pulled them out. The water came above my waist and it was cold. The water was about to the top of the wagon wheels. It was running pretty good and hard to stand up.

There was a big sand bar in the river and it pulled all of the horses. In fact I thought old Mike and Mark might not make it. They kind of struggled and floundered around and looked like they weren't going to pull their wagon through, but they did. That one wagon was the only one that didn't make it.

That was pretty early this morning and it was pretty cool. I wore my wet clothes, had no way to change clothes. The wind was a blowing. Then after our picture taking we came back out and crossed the river in the same crossing and everybody crossed all right that time.

When we crossed the river then, we stopped by the ranch buildings and Rosie the ranch cook there came out and she'd made up about 150 tacos and gave them to me so we ate tacos all day today. She's a Mexican cook that cooks there at the cookhouse for the Sun Ranch.

Then we came across the Sun Ranch to Split Rock. Tonight we'd just got into camp and I'd unhooked my horses and a real good friend that I had in John Day, Oregon, drove into camp. I spotted him so I walked over and we had a good visit. We had a awful lot of mosquitoes and bugs because we are traveling along the Sweetwater. A lot of dust. It was really dusty and dirty today.

William Riley Franklin in 1850 wrote:

WRF ∩ Camp 36, Monday 27th. Our caravan progressed 20 miles and encamped near Sweetwater. Here we found grass sufficient for our stock, artimesia (sage) covering perhaps thousands of acres, plenty for cooking purposes. The scenery of today's march was truly grand and magnificent to the curious and observing traveler. Mountains on either hand, to the left snowy peaks, to the right solid rock (granite) towering from 3 to 500 feet with scattering cedars and pine upon their sides and summits, growing in the crevices of the rock. In 5 miles of Independence Rock, we pass the "Devil's Gate." Here the river makes its way through a solid ridge of granite, the rock towering on either side 200 feet high above this, about 10 miles, is another gap through which the river winds its way, called the "Devil's Ladder." Those two last mentioned places have been generally considered not very desirable as the aforesaid individual is the great adversary of mans, but the places are truly grand and stupendous. Today we passed another lonely grave, silent and solitary abode, near the foot of a mountain, a truly Beautiful and apparently sacred place.

OF THE SAME REGION Edwin Bird in 1854 said: "I cannot describe it in more appropriate language than that it is Awful Sublime & Magnificent"

Hamilton Scott in his diary on July 5, 1862, wrote:
HS ∩ 1862. We laid in camp until one o'clock on account of Thomas Paul's wife being sick. She was better at noon so we hitched up. We have about eighty wagons in the train now. About five miles up the river we crossed, swimming our stock and pulling our wagons over a shaky bridge by hand. Drove three miles more up the river and camped near the Devil's Gate which the river runs through.

BETWEEN INDEPENDENCE Rock and South Pass in 1856 the greatest tragedy of the western migration occurred when two Mormon handcart companies became stranded in winter storms. The Willie and Martin Handcart Companies left winter quarters in Florence, Nebraska, too late in the season to make it across Wyoming before the weather turned bad. In mid-October 1856 the Saints struggled across snow-covered Wyoming.

"Every death weakened our forces. In my hundred I could not raise enough men to pitch a tent when we camped," John Chislett wrote as the party neared Independence Rock.

Between Devil's Gate and Split Rock, heavy snow stranded the Martin Company handcart pioneers. They took refuge in an area known now as Martin's Cove. A rescue brigade of Mormons from Salt Lake City who had learned of the companies' plight from missionaries who overtook the Willie and Martin Companies, arrived with supplies and took the people of Martin's Company on west in wagons. But some of the rescuers agreed to remain behind to guard the supplies and care for Mormon livestock left in the sheltered cove.

They ran short of food and nearly starved to death. Eventually they butchered the cattle, but still they had little food. They boiled the hides for whatever sustenance they might contain and were thinking of boiling the packsaddle when relief arrived in the spring. Many of the Martin Company died and are buried in Martin Cove, which is located on private property owned by the Sun family.

To the west of Martin Cove is Split Rock, a natural v-shaped formation in the Sweetwater Rocks. It is mentioned in trail diaries, but no vivid descriptions come from the emigrants. The distinctive v, serving as a marker for emigrants heading up the Sweetwater valley, became the most important landmark between Independence Rock and Oregon Buttes, visible for days as travelers journeyed around it.

In later years of trail travel, a stage, Pony Express, and telegraph station sat at Split Rock. Troops stayed there to protect the overlanders, at the emigrants called themselves particularly in the 1860s as Indian tribes finally rose against the travelers who flowed across the land.

When passing from Devil's Gate up the Sweetwater valley near Split Rock in 1854, Edwin Bird wrote:

EB ∩ Monday 19th [June]. This morning it was clear & very warm just as we were leaving camp Heavens artilary gave a morning salute off upon the bluffs where roas a black cloud In less than an hoar the sky was overspred the wind commenced to blow & a cold half rain half hale storm cam down upon us the contrast was great & we fairly suffered with the cold. the storm soon broke but it has been chilley all day & to knight is quite cold To day wee have been travling over hills back from the river & part of the time along the shore where we are camped to night The seanary has been fine have been in sight of snow all day also saw a natural road leading over the rockey bluffs which from where we were looked to be about twenty feet broad and thurty deep & as smoth as a floor

EB ∩ Tuesday 20th. The seanary has been beautiful beyond discription Upon every side could be seen high bluffs while off in the west the Sweet Watter mountains shrouded in its garb of perpetual winter appeared like a thing of beauty as the sun shone upon its snoey peaks it looked like an alabaster wall streching across our path whoes top seemed to touch the sky, where it sat enthroned in its beauty & grandure. Such a sight is seldom seen & when seen near [never] forgot"

EMIGRANTS FEARED THE Indians who were native to the land the overlanders crossed, but in reality white renegades caused more trouble than did the plains tribes. The western emigration intruded into the lives and lands of the Indian nations. They had different reactions, ranging from fear and hopelessness to aggression. The Indians didn't fear the emigrants, rather they feared the changes that came with the wagon travelers.

By the mid–1840s to early 1850s, the tribes knew some of the consequences associated with emigrant travelers. The greatest concerns were displacement, relocation, and disease. The Sweetwater River valley was traditional Shoshone territory, and as the emigrants moved through the region, Chief Washakie decided to let the travelers pass. A formidable warrior, he believed his people had more to gain by providing assistance.

Washakie hoped by allowing the emigrants to pass through his people's country unmolested, he could prevent fighting, retribution, and relocation.

Edwin Bird wrote Friday June 23, 1854:

EB ∩ 1854. This morning it was verey warm about 9 AM a fresh breas sprung up which made it verey plesant travling The road has been hard & gravaly but quite leval Crossed a branch of the Sweet Watter & Willow cricks which are verey clear swift streams about three rods wide & three feet deep upon the bank of the latter found a snow drift a number of us got a ball of it. Crossed the Sweet Watter about noon this is the last time we cross this stream as we near its source it is much clearer, colder & swifter This eavening we are camped upon the river and oposite of its snow mountains The Cheaf & a number of the Sheahocaneas or Snake Indians visited our camp when a rather curious circumstance happened & one which did not speak very well for our scalps Mr Parks had traded horses or rather a mule for an Indian Poney with the Cheafs Son in fitting the sturup strap he axadentally cut the young Blods fringes at once his wild Indian nature was aroused he sayed that a large company of his tribe were camped near us & that white men draw blud on an Indian good & sayed that he would come that knight & scalpe the whole train But Mr P—understanding them & knowing their love of money presented him with half a dollar which restored purfict friendship so much so that he wanted to embrace him.

The Split Rock stage, Pony Express and telegraph station, built in 1859 by William Russell, Alexander Majors, and William Waddell, lay deep in Shoshone country and escaped the wrath of the eastern and northern Indian tribes.

*Ben hitching Mark and Mike.* (Candy Moulton Photo)

But in March 1862, the traditionally friendly Shoshones went on the offensive, striking simultaneously at every station between Platte Bridge and Bear River in western Wyoming. Washakie's warriors did what other tribes had attempted for years. They shut down travel on the great Oregon road by cutting the telegraph link. Drivers, station attendants and guards, taken completely by surprise, saw the Indians capture every horse and mule belonging to the company in the area.

At President Lincoln's request, Brigham Young sent the Mormon Battalion—three hundred volunteers under the command of Captain Lot Smith—to quiet the Indians. The only killing in the uprising was that of a man at Split Rock who didn't understand when asked to prepare a meal. The Shoshones killed him and helped themselves to the larder.

**Ben Kern:**

BK July 18. It was real cold during the night. The wind blowed. We left Split Rock headed for Jeffrey City. Billy McIntosh came into camp this morning in his pickup about the time we were leaving and he asked Shawn and I if we wanted to be on the old original trail and we said we'd like to. He said, "If you got somebody with a pair of fence pliers put him in here with me and I'll put you on the old trail." When we got to his ranch, we pulled in by the ranch buildings and we went down and crossed the Sweetwater and he cut seven different fences today so we traveled on the old original ruts all day from there clear into Jeffrey City.

There was a couple of places where emigrants went out through the sandstone rims and the old ruts are embedded in the rocks there and they're very very plain. It was really sandy and it was slow going. It was sand from the time we left the Sun Ranch all the way up through here. As we traveled up the Sweetwater we saw the ruts and they're all very plain. There's probably 15 or 20 different wagon ruts wide where people spread out. They didn't follow each other because it was so dusty and dirty. You can see all the wagon ruts up through here.

We came to Jeffrey City. The people put us up at the football field. They built this nice school and field during the energy boom of the 1970s and 1980s, but the uranium market dropped and the people moved so the school doesn't have a team now.

Somewhere along the Sweetwater, William Riley Franklin and his train of thirteen wagons being pulled by Missouri mules, passed many gravesites. June 4, 1850, he wrote:

WRF 1850. Today we as usual passed several graves, woman's and man's. The lady died July 14, 1847. I acknowledge, kind reader, that this stirs my inmost soul and awakens the sympathies of my heart, makes many and curious reflection flit across my mind when I view so many graves and especially the grave of the gentle female so far off in the mountains and lonely and solitary wilds.

One strange curiosity along the Oregon Trail is Ice Slough or Ice Springs, located in a marshy area about midway between Jeffrey City and Sweetwater Station. Most emigrants headed west during the 1800s mentioned the spot. Irrigation drains the marsh more now and the ice no longer forms.

Ben Kern:

BK July 19. We left Jeffrey City headed for Sweetwater Station. I just hooked up and was getting ready to leave and Rosie the cook from the Sun Ranch brought me a whole bunch of Mexican food, delivered it to me. We went by Ice Slough. From the Ice Slough to Sweetwater Station we were on the old original trail. We had homemade bread and stew cooked by a woman who lives here by the river.

James A. Pritchard, on June 16, 1849, gave his view of the ice slough:

JP 1849. The Ice is found about 8 to 10 inches beneath the surface. Ther is from 4 to 6 inches of water above the Ice, and of turf or sod of grass appearantly floating on the water, upon which you can walk over it.... The water above the Ice is pretty strongly impregnated with Alkli. The upper end of the marsh is entirely that kind of water mixture. Tho there is good fresh water in spots. To get to the Ice you take a spade or Ax & cut away the sod & there strike down & cut it out in Squar blocks. The Ice is clear & pure entirely free from any Alkali and other unpleasant tast. It is from 4 to 10 inches thick, and as good as any I ever cut from the streams of Kentucky. I cut and filled my water bucket & took it with me.

Edwin Bird in 1854 wrote:

EB ∩ Wensday 21st [June]. To day it has been oppresively hot far more so than any we have had The most of the day we have been travling over a hard gravel road found no streams of watter for the releaf of our stock The greatest curiousity we have seen was the ice springs this is a low marshey looking place the ground looking very much like the breaking up of a winter at home there is but very little watter visable which upon the surface is quite warm but by runing your hand down it is distresingly cold Mr. Parks says that he has known species of ice two feet squar to have been taken out by diging down two or three feet & as clear as cristal The ground sprung & trembled as we passed over Undoubtedly this is an underground river & freases so hard in the winter that it forgets to thaw out The mountains that have been on eather side of us have asumed a smaller grade stretching away in hills.... We met several trains coming back to the states filled with mormans who sayed they had lived in the holey city long enough.

As wagons roll westward the grueling travel wears on nerves and tempers flare often. The long, hot days often led to conflicts. Hamilton Scott wrote in 1862:

HS ∩ July 6. Drove about twenty-five miles. No grass at noon. At four o'clock P.M. passed two trains camped who informed us of a murder committed near them today. Two men quarrled about a team, one shot the other, took his team and money. We travelled late, found no grass; cattle suffering for feed.

HS ∩ July 7. Started at sunrise, travelled four or five miles and found grass on river bottom. Several trains were camped here so we drove in and camped too. We are informed that the murderer is camped here. By request of some men from another camp, Captain Kennedy of our train ordered out twenty men, well armed to surround and take him, which they did. With court organized and a jury of twelve men selected, he was given a fair trial and a twelve to one verdict, guilty of willful murder. The prisoner kept under guard, we hitched up at two P.M. and drove eight miles.... A large train was camped here. Captain Kennedy called their whole company together and laid the case before them. They decided that the prisoner be executed tomorrow morning.

HS ∩ July 8. Gave prisoner his choice to be shot or hanged. He preferred to be shot. Twenty five armed men marched him one-half mile to where his grave had been prepared. Fourteen of the guns were loaded with bullets and the rest were blanks. When the signal was given they all fired, the prisoner falling backwards and dying within one minute. It was a sad sight to look upon. We immediately laid him in his grave without even a rough box. As soon as our work was completed, we moved on toward the setting of the sun.

ELIZABETH STEWART WARNER, in 1853 wrote, "They talk about the times that tried men souls but if thes ware not the times that tried both men and wemon's souls."

Discord struck in 1993, too. It was subtle and not seen by many of the people who rode for only a day or two with these wagons. After a few days on the hard plank seat it became more apparent. Although some of the tension resulted from disagreement over such seemingly mundane tasks as taking care of livestock and what time to leave camp in the morning, more of it involved personalities.

These people traveled together as closely as family. They had to rely upon each other to get through each and every day. Like any family living in close quarters and difficult circumstances, arguments broke out. So far as I know, there were only harsh words, no blows exchanged among the members of this train.

EARL LEGGETT:

EL We had rain, we had hail, we had snow, we had tornados, ...we had personality conflicts. You have personalities you can put together, but they never do mesh. We had days of rain, not just a little bit one day, it rained day in day out, night in night out in Nebraska and Kansas.

CANDY MOULTON:

CM I joined the wagons again on July 19, and traveled with them for several days. I met the train at Sweetwater Station. The wind blew hard all day, beating the moisture out of the land, and chapping lips and faces. The camp had a circle of eight or nine wagons, three tipis, and two small Army-style bivouac tents. I asked where to stow my gear and learned I would share one of the small tents with another woman.

I peered into the army tents and saw sleeping bags and backpacks. It was clear someone had already claimed them. I met Susan Anderson my tent companion, a Casper writer, whom I knew. The same photographer Zbysczek Bzdak was taking pictures for both of us on this trip and the three of us agreed to share sleeping accommodations so we threw our packs into one of the tipis, then headed our separate ways.

Eventually we decided to go to a cafe-bar in Jeffrey City to get something to eat for supper, and so Susan could retrieve her car. At the bar we hooked up with some of the seasoned crew on this wagon train. Dave Bowhay passed on one important piece of advice. It applied to today's wagon train participants, and it applied to those of the earlier migration: "If you see something laying in the road, stop and pick it up. You never know when you will need it."

Dave told of finding bailing wire and leather straps, of boards and buckles that came in handy.

The mosquitoes attacked in force as the sun dipped to the Wind Rivers in the west. Susan and I retreated to our tipi and found the mosquitoes beat us there. We also found a tent-mate; a woman who worked at the Wyoming State Training School in Lander. We told her there was one other person who would be sharing the tipi that night: a man. She didn't seem too concerned, and we appreciated her attitude.

After we slapped at mosquitoes and fanned them from our hands, faces and bodies, I resorted to chemical eradication and fogged the tent with mosquito spray. Almost immediately the pests disappeared, but we gagged on the smell of the insecticide.

As the lights went out, that is to say as the sun sank and dusk spread over the open land, we three women climbed into our sleeping bags. Zbysczek, pronounced like sfish shack, took care of his cameras and organized his film then, with full dark nearly upon us, prepared for bed. "I wonder if I should wear my nightshirt," he pondered aloud and we three women burst into gales of laughter.

Zbysczek is Polish and a true adventurer. He's traveled the Amazon from its source to the sea, has kayaked the world's wildest rivers, and has photographed in situations I can't even begin to imagine. Yet he packed his nightshirt and slipped it on as we settled among the sage in our canvas tipi which had tent poles made of plastic PVC pipe. A dirty blue plastic tarp covered the humps and clumps of sage, on which our sleeping bags lay.

We'd all barely settled into our bags when someone mentioned rattlesnakes and a discussion ensued about whether they would drift through the camp.

"I've heard they won't move onto northern slopes during the night," Lander said.

"They move all night," Susan replied.

"I think they won't come around where there is so much activity with people and horses and mules," I answered.

Zbysczek remained quiet.

We finally drifted to sleep with the reminder that a visitor could join us in the tipi as we dozed.

EARL LEGGETT:

EL What really was most impressive was that we didn't see any more rattlesnakes than we did, I don't know if it was because it was a wet year or not. I actually only seen two. One of 'em was when we was pulling in to Independence Rock and then the other one wasn't too far out of there, when we was out in the real sandy area.

BEN KERN:

BK July 20. We headed for McClean Meadows. We crossed the Sweetwater at Sweetwater Station. We couldn't get to McClean Meadows because the ground is too wet. Also the Rocky Ridge we'd have to pull to get out of the bottom would be awful hard on the teams and wagons. We came to Diamond Springs instead. We got into camp late.

CANDY MOULTON:

CM The wagons lined out of camp and a brisk breeze hit

us in the face as we made the fourth crossing of the Sweetwater River on the morning of July 20. A couple of black mules raced in a pasture just west of the crossing. Running free they seemed to want to join us as the wagons rolled by. Ben told his seatmate, a woman from Sweetwater Station who cooked dinner the previous night, he'd like to have those mules.

Shawn rode by on Ticky Tack, his mare, and a woman asked him if his backside gets sore. He told her he'd ridden nearly nine hundred miles since May 2 and if his butt wasn't hardened yet it never would be. An airplane buzzed the train, it was Zbysczek taking photos. The washboards in the road jangled our nerves and our bodies much of the day.

Just before lunch we headed up our first hill where we saw the clear swale of an old trail angling up a draw and over the rise. It is probably a route once used by freighters going to Atlantic City. The Rocky Ridge trail lay about three miles east of our route and the old emigrant trail ran even farther east on the Sweetwater itself.

The horses pulled hard as we climbed about 1,000 feet in elevation to camp at Diamond Springs. Most of the day we rode to the northwest of the trail ruts, but at times we caught glimpses of places where they mar the land. The sage grows higher at the edge of the trail swale. The rut itself is filled mostly with the fine western grama grasses, and little sage grew in the track. Those wispy clouds that presage wind, called mares' tails, whipped overhead in the sky today.

My back hurt when we reached camp from the pounding we took on the washboard road. As we traveled I noted some of the wildlife. Some gold finches, an antelope and fawn, prairie dogs, and a horned toad. We found a pocket knife in the road, and Dave stopped to pick it up. He gave it to Ben. Down the trail it might come in handy, just like he told us last night in Jeffrey City.

I shared the tipi with Lander and two young girls from Casper at our Diamond Springs camp. We halted up on a high knob in an area that looked like a natural spring had watered it earlier in the year. It had deep, lush, and green grass. The wagons parked in a straight line, rather than in a circle, because the tall sage and narrow location made it difficult to turn. Some of the people walked over the hill to an abandoned homestead, and others remained in camp. Donny Marincic spent his time in camp working on a painting of one of the wagon train participants. Donny has been with the train for several days, and will stay on through Western Wyoming.

BEN KERN:

BK July 21. Really cold this morning. I wished for those long johns I left back in Casper. Had a bad storm in the night. Thundered and lightninged. Didn't rain a whole lot. We left Diamond Springs heading for South Pass City. We stopped and had dinner at Rock Creek. After we left Rock Creek, we met the wagon train that does summer rides out of South Pass. We came down the grade into Atlantic City, which is really steep. This is the steepest hill we've encountered. Pretty steep pull from Atlantic City to South Pass City. That was a pretty steep grade coming out of there. Got into South Pass City. We will lay over here one day so we can work on wagons. We need to repair brakes and put some new springs under one wagon.

CANDY MOULTON:

CM The crash of thunder woke me in the night of July 20 as a storm moved around camp. When the first raindrops splatted against the tipi, I slipped out of my sleeping bag and went outside to close the top vent. If it rained hard we'd all get wet if it remained open. The lightning lit the sky and I heard voices from the other tents and tipis, a light shone from the wagon where Connie, who joined the train earlier in Wyoming, and Leeann slept. I returned to my bed and listened to the thunder, counting between crashes to see how far off it was. The crescendo gradually tapered and little rain fell.

I rode on the seat beside Ben as we pulled away from Diamond Springs. Our route swung around Rocky Ridge. In this area in 1856 the five hundred members of the Willie Handcart Company of Mormons had their greatest difficulties. Party leaders cut rations to conserve food as the Saints struggled through freezing streams, deep snows, piercing winds, and bitter temperatures. Snowflakes brushed their faces on October 19, the day leaders doled out the last of the flour.

Step after step the Saints forced themselves on until they camped in the willows at the Three Crossings of the Sweetwater. That night eighteen inches of snow fell, scattering their few starving draft animals in the storm. Dawn broke with five new corpses to be buried. They couldn't dig graves in the hard-frozen ground. Instead they buried the dead in a snowdrift. They struggled on.

John Chislett wrote: "Finally we were overtaken by a snowstorm which the shrill wind blew furiously about us. The snow fell several inches deep as we travelled along, but we dared not stop, for we had a sixteen-mile journey to make that day, and short of it we could not get wood and water."

As the company rested that noon, relief arrived. Missionaries from Salt Lake City brought supplies and said more were on the way. They told Willie to push on because the sixteen loads of provisions on the way from Fort Bridger would not last long for the fifteen hundred emigrants stranded—including those in his party and those of the Martin Company farther east. The Willie Company had little shelter, no wood, and the people hadn't eaten for two days. They were literally freezing and starving to death.

The Saints made the long difficult climb out of the Sweetwater valley and up Rocky Ridge. In the bitter cold, many frosted their hands, feet and faces because they didn't have proper clothing for the frigid temperatures. Relief arrived too late for many. Nine people died that night, and the next day, October 22, 1856, an additional fifteen people died. A mass grave holds their bodies.

Between sixty-two and sixty-seven members of the 500-person Willie Handcart Company died, as did an additional 135 to 150 members of the Martin Company, which traveled several days behind the Willie Company. Many people died with the independent Hodgett Wagon Train that same fall when they also became stranded by snow.

On our journey across their trail of despair, we followed an easy grade most of the day. Ben and I talked of people we knew in common and of riding bucking horses. He'd ridden them; I'd written about them. As we crossed the trail where the Willie Handcart pioneers had their most severe trials, we appeared taken back in time. The route was rough, a horse and wagon track where most vehicles couldn't go. The silence of the land seeped into us as we passed symbols of freedom: wild horses and sheepherder monuments.

A small group of wild horses watched us from one ridge and Ben told me it was a stud herd. The old stud, a big bay, had a tail that nearly touched the ground, giving an indication of his age. The horses made no move to approach our wagons, but watched, perhaps in wonder, at the strange contraptions passing by. None of the horses in the train created any problems, although they cocked their ears and closely watched as we drove by the wild ones.

We took a break at Rock Creek, where fifteen members of the Willie Company lie in their eternal slumber. Those who

*"Mormon Party Near Fort Bridger" by William Henry Jackson. The 1856 exodus of the Latter Day Saints was primarily made with the use of handcarts. These carts were relatively easy to use and repair but limited the amount of goods that could be transported. When they reached Fort Bridger, near the present-day border between Wyoming and Utah, their journey was nearing its end.* (Courtesy Scotts Bluff National Monument)

died here ranged in age from six-year-old Jens Nilson to James Gibb, age sixty-seven.

I offered a prayer of thanksgiving at this special place. My husband's family traveled with the Willie Company. His great-great grandfather was one of the three babies born during the migration. Charles Moulton's birth took place on *The Thornton* just as it sailed into the Irish Sea. Until the family reached Utah, they carried Charles on a pillow because he was so frail.

As they struggled over Rocky Ridge, one of the Moulton children, five-year-old Heber, froze his hand in the bitter temperatures and he later lost several fingers. If the Moulton family hadn't left England with the handcart emigrants, I might not have my husband Steve and my own two children Shawn and Erin Marie and I can't imagine life without them.

A lot of people must visit the monument. Some enterprising man was running a concession stand on the creek bank. He sold pop and candy bars. A sign advertised the place for sale, so maybe business wasn't all that good. Ben and I shared a Pepsi as Mark and Mike began the short climb out of Rock Creek. Piles of dirt along the banks of the creek provided a reminder of mining operations that once claimed this region.

We veered from the trail to head to South Pass City. Just as the horses used their power to pull us up hills yesterday, today they strained to hold the wagons back as we switchbacked down into Atlantic City. The side backer harnesses used on these wagons put the pressure on the horses' hindquarters as they hold the wagons back.

Going down hills the drivers used their brakes by putting a foot against a rope tied to the brake handle. As we rolled down that steep hill, Leeann broke her brake rope. She held the team back while outrider Dave Bowhay jumped from his horse to the wagon and pulled the brake lever. Then outriders put a specially designed rough-lock shoe on one back wheel. That kept the wheel from turning so the wagon skidded rather than rolled. As Dave held the brake, Leeann continued driving the team down the hill. With the rough-lock on, the horses then had to pull the wagon, rather than hold it back.

BEN KERN:

BK July 22. When we got up this morning it was cold. The ground was white, it was really Frosty. Left South Pass City headed for Pacific Springs. We crossed the Sweetwater twice this morning. We had lunch on the Continental Divide. Mary Hay rode with us and we were out on the top of South Pass and she got off way out there and just took off afoot and walked back to her ranch.

We crossed the Continental Divide. I feel like we will succeed in accomplishing our journey. I feel like we definitely will finish our trip. I just feel like we really accomplished something, when we crossed over the Continental Divide, especially after all the things we've already went through.

Got into Pacific Springs fairly early in the afternoon, but before we got into camp it started raining. It was so muddy when we got into camp. Really had a bad storm, it rained on us, thundered and lightninged.

South Pass became the key to the Oregon migration. It is a broad saddle in the Rocky Mountains noted by the Astorians in 1812, by mountain man Thomas Fitzpatrick in 1824, and marked by John C. Frémont in 1842. Historically Oregon lay beyond the pass. October 22 burned in my mind. On that date in 1812, Stuart and his men first crossed South Pass. On that day in 1856 the great deaths on the Willie Handcart Company occurred. I remember the day easily. It is my birthday.

South Pass is the single most important feature on the Oregon Trail. Without it there might have been no trail across Wyoming.

EARL LEGGETT:

EL It was good to see a hill, but you wanted to see it all at one time. I was really surprised by the incline that we had here, I could see you needed to get here and not tarry too long. This is July. We had snow and ice here, it was 28 degrees. This time of year there's a great temperature change from nighttime to high noon. It has a lot to do with the altitude and the air currents.

CANDY MOULTON:

CM It was very cold when we pulled out of South Pass City. The water buckets had ice on them. The wind washed off the snow-covered Wind River mountains to the north. I pulled my hat down low and zipped my down-filled coat to my neck. I found a pair of gloves in my bag this morning and I needed them. My fingers tingled with the cold and I recalled how Heber Moulton's fingers froze as he climbed Rocky Ridge in 1856. He had no gloves for protection.

We took a lunch break near some abandoned farm buildings, but didn't linger too long. It was too cold to stand idly by. I sat with Ben as we waited for the wagons to get ready to roll. Mike pawed the ground and tried to lie down, even though he was hitched to Mark. Ben tapped him lightly with a short nylon whip and shook the lines. He talked to the horse in a soothing voice.

"I think he has a belly-ache," Ben told me. Moving would help ease it, and Ben was anxious to get back on the trail. The wind became colder and I took the Indian-style blanket I'd been sitting on and placed it over my legs and Ben's. We huddled together in the wind as our wagon moved toward the South Pass markers. I wished I had on my long underwear.

We crossed the Sweetwater twice. The first time it wasn't deep. The second time near the river's edge we crossed a wide area that had huge bog bumps. The wagons rocked and rolled over the big humps, making the roughest ride so far on the trip. When we reached the river itself, the land smoothed out. The water didn't reach the horses' knees, still it splashed to near the bottom of the wagon bed. Ben held firm control as we rolled over the river boulders and up the steep bank on the far side.

Rancher Mary Hay rode with us today. She walked ahead of the wagons part of the time, her stride the smooth, loose movements of a woman used to traveling in the open. We were driving across an unenclosed sage area and could see nothing man-made anywhere around when Mary told Ben, "Thanks for the ride." Then she climbed over the back tailgate of the wagon, jumped to the ground, and quickly got out of the trail so she wouldn't be in the way of Marie's team, which closely followed Ben.

Mary tugged her brown hat low over her forehead and with her sandy-brown braids bouncing against her shoulders, took off across the plains. It seemed funny to see her striding toward a home we couldn't see.

Indians used South Pass long before white men, crossing from campsites in the Wind River Valley where they spent their winters, to the broad Green River valley and its abundant hunting resources. The Stuart Party gets the credit for discovery of South Pass by white men in 1812 as they returned from Fort Astoria, Oregon.

The pass saw little use from whites until the 1820s. Thomas Fitzpatrick of the Rocky Mountain Fur Company in 1824 chanced upon the pass, which he reported to General Ashley. It offered a wide grassy gateway to the Green River valley and the various trapping spots of the West: Pierre's Hole, Colter's Hell, the Three Forks of the Missouri, Bear Lake, Cache valley, Ogden's Hole, and Great Salt Lake valley.

In 1827 Ashley sent a four-pounder cannon drawn by four mules through the pass, and in 1832 Captain Benjamin Bonneville took the first wagons over. When missionaries Marcus Whitman and Samuel Parker crossed South Pass in 1835, Parker, not dreaming that the most mountainous country lay west of the divide, noted in his journal that "there will be no difficulty in constructing a railroad from the Atlantic to the Pacific."

Trappers and traders used the pass until 1841 when the first wagon train crossed the broad swale. In the late 1850s the stagecoach provided faster transportation over the Oregon Trail route and South Pass. By 1860, the Pony Express of Russell,

*A marker at South Pass commemorating the crossing of Narcissa Prentiss Whitman and Eliza Hart Spalding in 1836.* (Candy Moulton Photo)

Majors, and Waddell crossed the pass. Creighton replaced the short-lived Pony Express with a telegraph he built in 1861.

South Pass is a twenty-five-mile wide, long treeless valley broken by low flat-topped sagebrush hills and pyramidal sand dunes. Old wagon tracks are so numerous that the valley resembles an aged plowed field. The incline on both approaches is so gradual it is difficult to determine the actual divide.

Theodore Talbot, on Aug. 22, 1843, wrote: "Today we set foot in Oregon Territory…'The land of promise' as yet only promises an increased supply of wormwood and sand."

Elizabeth Geer wrote August 1, 1847: "Passed over the Rocky Mountains, the backbone of America. It is all rocks on top and they are split into pieces and turned up edgewise. Oh, that I had time and talent to describe this curious country. We wound over the mountains along a very crooked road."

William Riley Franklin in 1850, wrote:

WRF ∩ Camp 40, Friday 31 [May]. This day a march brought us to the famous south pass of the Rocky Mountains.... This pass of which you have doubtless often heard, is no more than an inclined plain, or dividing ridge between the waters of the Pacific and Gulf of Mexico, and here all emigrants to Oregon and California pass into the Rocky Mountains. The waters of salt springs run into Green River, thence, Sacramento, thence the Pacific, hence its name. This pass or dividing ridge was to us what the Rubicon was to Caesar and his army.

Edwin Bird wrote in 1854:

EB ∩ 1854. This morning it was clear & very warm Here we left the Sweetwatter & its mountains to the right after travling a short distance we came to the sumit of the Rockey Mountains All the watter east of this emties into the Mississippi its tributaries & the Gulf of Mexico All west into the Great Basin where the most of it sinks There was so much romance conected with the place, The theme of poets & novelists that made it very interesting How often had I wished to visit this celabrated range & to stand upon its disey top but how my yuthful fances faded I was not a notch higher than all creation I did not stand upon an elevation that would enable me to look down upon valies rivers & sparkling cascades but where ever I turned my eyes could be seen still higher peaks But how many have longed to feas their eye upon the grandure of this place & how many have started with high hope of reaching these wild reagans but have found an early grave & the rude slab here & there tells where lies their sleeping ashes.... In memory of the place I picked up three small stones, And waved a last adue to the Atlantic States & the Atlantic slope

At Pacific Springs modern day traveler Christina Holbrook, 9, of Casper wrote for an article in the *Casper Star-Tribune:*

CH Even though I've been on the wagon for just a few days... it seems like a life time. Although it's very fun there are many things to do, learn and also see, but when you're riding on a wagon it can get boaring and tiring. The most interesting part of the trip was when we fored the [Sweetwater] river and our stay at South Pass City.

CANDY MOULTON:

CM We camped at Pacific Springs, west of South Pass. It rained most of the night. Susan returned to Casper so Zbysczek and I shared a tent. The rain poured down when we pulled into camp, and Ben told me to be sure to get one of the Army-style bivouac tents. Those small tents have floors and zippered-doors that can be tightly shut. That makes them both warmer and drier. I told the two Casper girls they should get one as well and I saw them with their bags by the door before anyone else.

I peeled off my boots and pants just after stepping into the tent because they were caked with red gumbo mud. Awful stuff.

I crawled into my sleeping bag long before Zbysczek came in. I didn't hear him come into the tent. He visited late. We rolled out at 6 A.M. to find the ground outside our tents a slick, slimy gumbo. The heavens had cried all night.

As the wagons pulled away from Pacific Springs, the sky lay heavy, the clouds just barely above the dirty, once-white canvas wagon coverings. It was perfectly still, a rarity in Wyoming, and quiet. Unlike other mornings, people didn't talk and visit.

I closed my eyes and felt the pounding of the hard plank wagon seat as we bounced over mountain sod and sage. The fresh aroma of crushed sagebrush assailed my nose as I listened to creaking wagon wheels, the soft jangle of horse harnesses, and an occasional murmur from Ben to Mark and Mike. It seemed almost as if we would shatter the spell and power of the moment if we spoke.

All day we drove the ruts, stopping only once. Phil and Donny Marincic cut a highway right-of-way fence because there was no other way to get through. We crossed the pavement and they repaired the fence, then we again moved away from modern contrivance.

I could easily imagine what the trail had been like for the pioneers as we rolled from False Parting of the Ways. Modern man's leavings don't clutter the route by Plume Rock. The pickup with the portable bathrooms, the National Guard water truck that traveled with the train through Wyoming to provide fresh water, and the tourists didn't follow us on these ruts. Drizzling rain dripped from the wagon covering, but no breeze fanned our faces, and we could hear only soft voices as people talked, the jangle of horse harnesses, and the creaking of the wagon.

Plume Rock beckoned, and a Bureau of Land Management interpretive sign told us its story. All afternoon the only sign of modern man was that granite marker. If it hadn't marked the trail, we could have easily believed we'd time-traveled. We saw no vehicles, no power lines, no roads, no other people, and because of the clouds, not even any jet contrails.

We drove on a two-track road most of the day that was the original trail. Sometimes we saw other ruts to the side of our paths. The BLM gave permission for the wagons to be on the ruts. Not all, but some BLM employees strongly support wagon travel on original ruts because that maintains the trails in a natural way. In one place just before Phil and Donny cut the fence, a highway construction project had destroyed the original trail ruts. When we crossed that section we restored the trail by driving on it with only wagons, or by riding horses over the land.

The temperature dropped and clouds hugged the Wind Rivers. We pulled blankets and tarps around us to remain somewhat dry as misty rain turned the trail sloppy.

We had a view of sage, bitterbrush and four remarkable sets of parallel ruts. The landscape had changed little during the past one hundred and fifty years. I found myself counting the landmarks I'd passed: Rock Creek Station, Ogallala, California Hill, Chimney Rock, Independence Rock, Split Rock, Ice Slough, Rocky Ridge, South Pass, Pacific Springs, Plume Rock. I thought of those landmarks still ahead on the road to Oregon.

West of South Pass this land hasn't changed much since the Great Migration. The area took its toll on the spirits of men, women and children, and it weighed heavily upon the backs of the oxen or horses pulling the wagons. A lack of good feed, combined with poor water often resulted in devastating effects. The alkali ate away at boots and shoes, if overlanders were lucky enough to have a pair remaining on their tired and sore feet. And it burned their eyes and noses.

The travelers wrote of dust in their eyes and of having difficulty breathing because of the smell of dead oxen and cow dung. They had to keep stock from drinking alkali water, which will kill people or animals.

To ease the discomfort of the stock, travelers washed the animals' noses with fresh water, and when the stock became ill from drinking the alkali, they poured lard and vinegar down them to effect a cure.

**Ben Kern:**

BK July 23. We left Pacific Springs, headed for Parting of the Ways and it rained on us all day today.

BK July 24. It rained all night. We left Parting of the Ways headed for Farson, still raining. Awful muddy. Had a wedding this morning before we pulled camp. Got into Farson early afternoon and then we will lay over at Farson for two days. We want to go look at some mules that are for sale.

CANDY MOULTON:

CM The muddy ground at Parting of the Ways, caused Zbysczek and I to decide we would camp at the Oregon Trail Motel in Farson. We got a thirty-two dollar room, then headed to the Oregon Trail Bar where we met Connie and Donny. Ben and several others from the wagon train joined us. We made business telephone calls and then spent the evening, into the early hours of the morning, engaged in serious trail talk.

Somewhere between the beer and wine and whiskey, we ordered meals: steak and hamburgers. Zbysczek made arrangements to fly over the train at dawn with a local pilot, who said he could land on the muddy road. We told him he'd get stuck for sure. The town of Farson had planned a big celebration for the arrival of the wagon train and among the events was a Pony Express race. We decided Connie should enter and represent the train. As we headed to our beds, we felt confident she could win.

When Zbysczek and I rented our room for the night, the woman at the motel handed me a pitcher of water and told me to drink the water in the pitcher and not that from the tap. Hours later I let the warm water of a shower wash away trail grime and felt slimy as I stepped from the shower. I noticed that my silver necklace was tarnished black by the alkali in the water.

Zbysczek left before dawn for his flight over the wagons. I met him several hours later for breakfast at the Oregon Trail Restaurant. Over bacon and eggs we talked of the flight. His pilot had indeed set the plane down on the muddy road, just in time for Zbysczek to attend the wedding. As we ate, a man in a black suit with a carnation on his lapel walked by the restaurant.

"That's the groom," Zbysczek told me. "You ought to go interview him."

I abandoned breakfast and headed out the door after the man, who'd gone into the Oregon Trail Bar. He had a six-pack of beer under his arm as I asked him about the wedding. He told me he and his bride decided to get married at "Parting of the Ways" because they thought it was a sentimental place.

As Zbysczek and I headed back toward Casper, we had difficulty leaving the train behind, and decided to take more photos near Parting of the Ways. Zbysczek drove my four-wheel-drive Subaru, and I opened the gates as we raced across the sandy soil and sagebrush to catch the train. Although we knew where we should have been able to find them, we didn't spot the white sails of the wagon tops until we reached Dry Sandy.

The Subaru wouldn't get us any closer, so we took off on foot, slipping down the sagebrush lined banks and struggling through the deep sandy stream bed. At the other side, we clearly saw the wagons, heading toward us and we sat down on the bank to wait for them. They dipped and rolled across the waves of the trail, following the ruts carved a century and a half ago. As each wagon passed us by, we called greetings and waved. Connie drove one wagon, so we knew she wouldn't ride in the Pony Express race at Farson as we'd planned the night before, because the race would be over before the wagons got to town. The wagons turned away from us as they neared the historic parting spot.

At the time of the great migration, Oregon started at the Continental Divide marked by the barely-discernable South Pass. The first striking natural feature to the west is Oregon Buttes. In July 1844 the California-bound Stevens-Townsend-Murphy wagon train guided by Isaac Hitchcock and 81-year-old Caleb Greenwood headed due west from South Pass

*Pinedale, Wyoming, rancher Phil Marincic drives his team of white horses on a different route as the sesquicentennial wagon train nears Parting of the Ways in western Wyoming.* (Candy Moulton Photo)

crossing about fifty miles of semi-arid desert, first passing close to the present-day town of Farson, rejoining the trail at Cokeville.

Their path veered from the route most westward-bound emigrants traveled, and it saved about five or six day's traveling time by taking a more direct course. The route eliminated the need to travel eighty-five miles south to Fort Bridger and then northwest to present-day Cokeville. However, the trade-off was a fifty mile waterless stretch between the Little Sandy River and the Green River.

Many Forty-Niners seeking their fortune in the California Gold Rush, followed this shorter route, first known as the Greenwood Cutoff. Of the estimated thirty thousand Forty-Niners traveling the Oregon Trail, nearly two-thirds or some twenty thousand used the Greenwood Cutoff. Due to an error in the 1849 Joseph E. Ware Guidebook, the Greenwood route then became known as the Sublette Cutoff.

It split from the old established trail at a location often called the "Parting of the Ways." However, in reality the primary trail to California and Oregon didn't part until it reached the Wyoming-Idaho border. Thus sometimes the forking spot of Greenwood Cutoff is referred to as the False Parting of the Ways.

Several other versions of the cutoff pioneered during the western migration include the Kinney, Slate Creek and Dempsey-Hockaday cutoffs. They all headed roughly west from Farson to Cokeville. The sesquicentennial train followed the main trail, not any of the cutoffs.

The cutoffs gave the trail a braided look—much as it has in eastern Nebraska—with many sets of ruts across the landscape. The travelers taking any of the cutoffs had to contend with the dry stretch. They camped by day and started their journey in the evening, driving through the night and all the next day. By the second evening they reached the Green if they maintained a walking pace of about two miles per hour.

Frederick W. Lander supervised construction of the Lander Cutoff in 1858. It went from Rocky Ridge east of South Pass to Fort Hall, Idaho, to provide a shorter emigrant route. Officially, the route was the Fort Kearny, South Pass and Honey Lake Road.

Lander, a powerfully-built man, was at South Pass July 15, 1857, with a party of fourteen, including six engineers, to begin exploring the wagon route. By the end of summer he had explored sixteen mountain passes, defined topography of the Wasatch Mountain chain, and discovered several practical wagon routes.

The route he preferred went from South Pass along the Sandy and Green Rivers to Thompson Pass. It entered Idaho, crossed the headwaters of the Blackfoot and Portneuf Rivers, and continued to Ross Fork. Lander liked the route because of the availability of grass, timber, and pure water. Fish and game were plentiful, and he thought the route could also possibly serve for the location of a railroad line.

Eleven months after he first stood at South Pass, on June 14, 1858, Lander started construction of the wagon road. His construction crew included Mormon laborers, lumbermen, and bridge builders from Maine who dug, chopped, and blasted their way into Idaho, building fifteen miles of road a day.

A letter, probably written by somebody working to improve the Lander Cutoff, while at the crossing of Green River July 6, 1859, said: "Yesterday was a most tedious day to all the party. We had to cross Green River a rushing mountain torrent about fifty or sixty yards wide and with a current so strong as to take the animals from their feet.... While I write one of the men tells me that an emigrant wagon has been swept down the stream, poor man he lost all of his provisions and many other things of great value to him."

Illness and death were common on the trail with large numbers of people dying of Asiatic Cholera in Nebraska. The third largest number of deaths during the migration is attributed to accidents and only about four hundred people lost their lives as a result of attack by Indians.

There is no documented evidence that any Indian attacks ever took place involving a circled-up Oregon Trail wagon train; that is a scene fabricated by Hollywood. In the Mountain Meadows Massacre that occurred away from the trail in southern Utah, Indians did attack a circled train, but Mormons instigated and led their action.

**Ben Kern:**

BK July 27. Left Farson for Simpson's Hollow. It rained

on us again. It was really muddy. Phil Marincic was leading us and we were going to follow the old original trail, we pulled out, but it was so muddy we had to go back to the highway

BK July 28. We left Simpson's Hollow and headed for Green River Station. We had to be at the Green River at 11 o'clock for the dedication for the Lombard Ferry. Then we went back across the river and decided we would ford the river. Went across the Green where the original trail crossed. I was the first wagon that went across and I made it over.

At one time Mark and Mike were swimming and the wagon was pulling, floating downstream real bad, but I made it across. I kept 'em a going. I didn't let 'em slack off and I made 'em look for the other side. The water was to their bellies in most places, and deep enough to make them swim. It was swift, I really noticed that. The bank on this side of the river is really steep, the horses was really down and pulling to get up on the bank.

In some areas there's big boulders in the river, where people have hauled them in and dumped to keep the bottom of the river from eroding and washing away. When Leeann's team broke away from her wagon, I was on Ticky Tack and I picked Maggie and Molly up when they pulled the running gears away from her wagon. That's when I noticed how swift the water was, when I went back in there. The water was about up to my knees as I rode Ticky Tack into the current. We made camp along the Green River. We are right on the bank of the Green River, real pretty campsite.

THE GREATEST THRILL in 1993 came in crossing the Green River. Ben crossed without problems, but two of the wagons had difficulty. This is the way Leeann told the story to the *Casper Star-Tribune*: "Then it's my turn. Me and Kris really wanted to go across the Green River. I was going along pretty steady, we had drifted really far down river. I pulled [the team] left a little. We felt this clunk, clunk, we were going over rocks. Pretty soon the horses were swimming."

As Leeann handled the lines she talked to her team. "Maggie, Molly come on" she said as she felt them get their traction. But when they pulled, a pin came loose from the bottom of her wagon and that allowed the front wheels to pull free, separating the team from the wagon. "I felt the lines slide right through my hands."

Leeann and Erin, her only passenger, climbed to the high side of the wagon. "We saw water starting to run through my wagon…a bunch of stuff was just floating down the river…. I'm watching stuff floating down the river and my wagon and I thought, oh, this is fun. I wasn't too scared. If I started getting into the water I would have started getting scared. I just knew I was under control so I wasn't scared."

Leeann got a ride out of the river on the back of a horse and the Wyoming Army National Guard truck pulled her wagon free. "I slept in it that night. It smelled like moss."

Emigrants either forded or had their wagons and stock ferried across the Green River (Rio Verde) in western Wyoming. The Oregon Trail crossed the Green River in numerous places and ferries operated at many sites. Unlike the North Platte at Casper, which eventually had bridges across its width, the Green remained free flowing and a difficult obstacle. Early western-bound travelers forded the Green River at the mouth of Steed Canyon, south of LaBarge Creek. The crossing was a little more than a mile northeast of Names Hill.

In late June 1847 Mormons built a ferry across the Green roughly a half-mile downstream from the Sublette Crossing. John B. Hill in July 1850 noted that the Mormon Ferry operator "allowed too many passengers to get into the boat, and the water came within two inches of the gunwale." The ferryman ordered the men to stay still as he continued moving the ferry across the river. When the ferry neared the far side of the river it dipped and water washed over the boat. Hill wrote, "[a] few of us jumped to the lower side of the boat, and it was righted at once.... At that time Green River was booming."

Bryarly Wakeman, a member of the Charleston Company from Virginia, reached Sublette's Crossing July 2, 1849, where he found many wagons waiting to cross on the ferry. The French ferry owner charged eight dollars to take a load over the river. Generally it took three such trips to cross with a wagon-load of goods. Wakeman reported the Green River as being one hundred and fifty yards wide and about ten feet deep. He said it had a strong current.

In 1850 William Riley Franklin, wrote:

WRF ∩ Camp 41, Saturday. June 1st. We marched 23 miles over a very good road and encamped in about a mile of Big Sandy, where we found first rate grass for this country.

WRF ∩ Camp 42, Sunday the 2nd. We rested and grazed our mules until 2 o'clock, then watered them, filled our kegs with water and started into a desert of 40 miles. We progressed about 10 miles and halted and let our mules graze about 2 hours, then set forward and traveled until 2 o'clock in the night, making 15 miles. Here we encamped for the remainder of the night. This night our caravan took another general stampede doing no injury at all.

Edwin Bird wrote in 1854:

EB ∩ Tuesday 27th [June]. To day it is clear & warm left the big sandy and crossed over to Green River this stream is bout one quarter of a mile wide is damp & very swift runing about seven miles the hour There is a ferrey & several log houses located here At present there are a great many waiting to cross the teams & tents form quite a vilage with I should judge five hundred inhabitents Yesterday a man was drowned while trying to swim the river on horse, he leaves a Wife & two Children to morn his loss To knight we re camped on the east side about one & a half miles from the ferrey The seanary upon this stream is very grand the cotton wood grows quite large & the flats are rich in soil while the turbid river flows on & helps to swell the waughters of Colorado the Sweet Waughter mountains are still in sight

EB ∩ Wednesday 28th. This morning it was clear & warm started at an early hour to swim our stock While we were wating for a drove to get out of the way a thunder storm came up in the west accompanyed by a high wind the hevest of the storm passed around but it raned quite hard for a few minutes In four trials we suckceded in geting our stock acrost the current was swift & cold so that it took the anamels down stream for half a mile before they ganed the oposite shore Whol treas came down which would make cords of wood We ferried our wagons acrost without axident & camped on the west shore for the rest of the day I picked up 3 small but very prety stones one was a very prety agott to keep in remembrence of Green River Near us to night are several companies camped therfore the order or bill of the eavning has been singing dancing & storey telling

**Ben Kern:**

BK July 29. We left the Green River headed for Granger. This was a very long day. We had 23 miles. We are camped at the park in Granger and the community put on a feed for us.

*Ben Kern moves his team across the sage-covered ground in western Wyoming.* (Candy Moulton Photo)

BK July 30. We left Granger and made it to Lyman. I had some errands to run and when I got into camp the mountain men out of Lyman or Fort Bridger had come in and kidnapped people as a fun re-creation. They were having a dance in the middle of the road when I got into camp.

ALTHOUGH THE Forty-Niners intent on getting to California as quickly as they could, took the dry cutoff from Farson to Big Sandy, by far the majority of Oregon-bound travelers headed south on the primary trail. Their route went to Fort Bridger established in 1842 by Jim Bridger "in the path of the emigrants."

Emigrants used three major outfitting points between the Missouri River and the Pacific: Fort Laramie, Fort Bridger, and Fort Hall. Historian Hiram Chittenden classed Fort Bridger as the first trader's post west of the Mississippi ever built for the "convenience of emigrants."

"These two landmarks—the return of Lewis and Clark, and the founding of Fort Bridger—determine the limits of a distinct period in western history," Chittenden wrote.

Jim Bridger was born in 1804 in Richmond, Virginia. In 1822 he came west with the fur brigade of General William H. Ashley. Although illiterate, Bridger learned the fur trade from Ashley and served as a right-hand man under Jedediah S. Smith, William L. Sublette, and David E. Jackson from 1826 to 1830.

Bridger joined with Milton Sublette, Thomas Fitzpatrick, Henry Fraeb, and John Baptiste Gervais to form the Rocky Mountain Fur Company in 1830. Bridger worked with the American Fur Company, founded by John Jacob Astor along with Lucien Fontenelle and Andrew Drips, his former competitors, from 1836 to about 1843.

Bridger first saw the Blacks Fork of the Green River when he trapped for Ashley. He discovered the Salt Lake valley in 1824, told great stories about the geysers and other natural wonders of the Yellowstone area, and made a reputation as a trapper, guide, and scout.

But beaver was out of style by 1842, and the streams were nearly trapped out anyway. Bridger and his Indian wife took up residence on the banks of Black's Fork to await the emigrants.

In a letter from Bridger but almost certainly written for him by someone else to Pierre Choteau Jr., head of a fur and trading company in St. Louis, dated December 10, 1843, Bridger said:

JB ∩ 1843. I have established a small fort, with a blacksmith shop and a supply of iron in the road of the emigrants on the Black Fork of Green River, which promises fairly. In coming out here they are generally well supplied with money, but by the time they get here they are in need of all kinds of supplies, horses, provisions, smithwork, etc. They bring ready cash from the states, and should I receive the goods ordered, will have considerable business in that way with them, and establish trade with the Indians in the neighborhood, who have a good number of beaver among them. The fort is a beautiful location on Black's Fork of Green River, receiving fine, fresh water from the snow on the Uintah Range. The streams are alive with mountain trout. It passes the fort in several channels, each lined with trees, kept alive by the moisture of the soil.

Bridger's trading partner, Louis Vasquez, may have been an Ashley man in 1822. Vasquez probably devoted more of his time to the trading end of the partnership than did Bridger.

William G. Johnston in *Experiences of a Forty-niner*, described Vasquez as a "fine, portly looking gentlemen of medium height, about 50 years of age, and making an impression of being intelligent and shrewd."

John Wilson, Indian agent at "Saltlake, California," in 1849 called Vasquez and Bridger "gentlemen of integrity and intelligence, and can be fully relied on in relation to any statement they make in regard to the different tribes, claims, and other information in relation to the Utah and Sho-Sho-Nie tribes."

Bridger didn't have a spectacular fort. On July 25, 1845, Joel Palmer described the place:

JP ∩ 1845. It is built of poles and daubed with mud; it is a shabby concern. Here are about twenty-five lodges of Indians, or rather white trappers' lodges occupied by their Indian wives. They have a good supply of robes, dressed deer, elk and antelope skins, coats, pants, moccasins, and other Indian fixens, which they trade low for flour, pork, powder, lead, blankets, butcher-knives, spirits, hats, ready-made clothes, coffee, sugar,

> etc. They ask for a horse from twenty-five to fifty dollars in trade. Their wives are mostly of the Pyentes and Snake Indians. They generally abandon this fort during the winter months. At this place the bottoms are wide, and covered with good grass. Cotton wood timber in plenty. The stream abounds with trout.

Edwin Bryant supported that view when he wrote on July 17, 1846:

> EB ∩ 1846. The buildings are two or three miserable log cabins, rudely constructed, and bearing but a faint resemblance to habitable houses. Its position is in a handsome and fertile bottom of the small stream on which we are encamped, about two miles south of the point where the old wagon trail, via Fort Hall, makes an angle and takes a northwesterly course.

Hundreds of wind-swept, dry, dusty miles separated Fort Laramie and Fort Bridger. By the time overlanders arrived at Bridger's fort on the Blacks Fork of the Green, they needed to rest and recuperate. And Bridger was right; they needed supplies.

Unfortunately, emigrants didn't always find the supplies they needed. Vasquez often went for prolonged rides in the countryside in a coach and four, while Bridger, who went by the nickname, Old Gabe, had a wanderlust that never ceased. They didn't tend to business as prudently as they might have.

When Bridger settled at the fort in 1842, Mexico held the territory. But following the Mexican War, Mexico in 1848 ceded the land to the United States. Bridger owned the fort from 1843 until 1853, when it went into Mormon hands. The Mormons and Brigham Young claimed they bought the fort for $8,000. Bridger always said they stole it.

The Mormons had growing power and wealth and encountered increasing hostility from the federal government, according to R.S. Ellison in *A Brief History of Fort Bridger*. They may have threatened and coerced Bridger into selling his fort thereby removing it as a launching point for non-Mormons to reach the gateway to the Great Salt Lake valley.

In an October 27, 1873, letter to Senator Benjamin F. Butler, Bridger said Mormons under Young's direction robbed him and threatened him with death. Bridger said the Mormons took merchandise, livestock and other possessions—allegedly amounting to more than $100,000. He claimed the Mormons partially destroyed his buildings and that he barely escaped with his life.

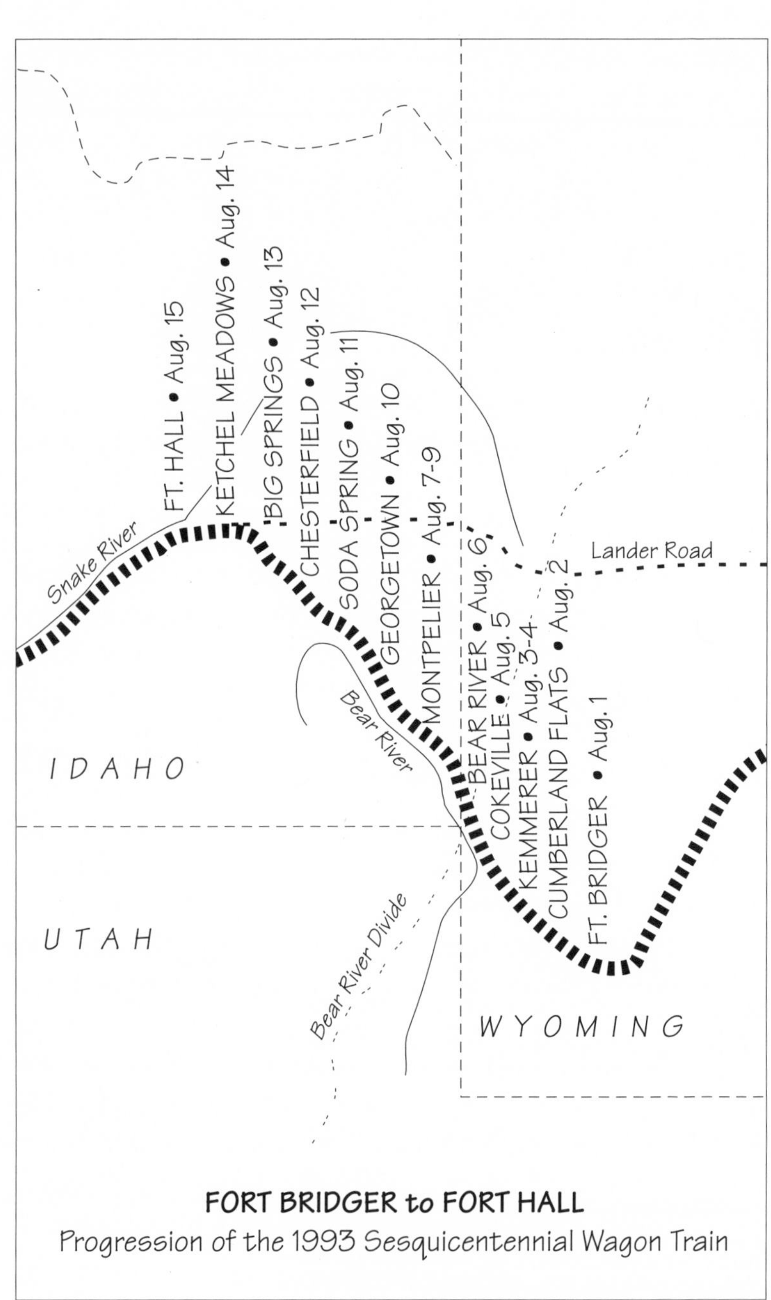


**FORT BRIDGER to FORT HALL**

Progression of the 1993 Sesquicentennial Wagon Train

PART SIX:

# Fort Bridger to Fort Hall

*You can always sell a horse man on a mule,*
*but you can never sell a mule man on a horse.*
—Earl Leggett, 1993

Fort Bridger, Wyoming. Oregon-bound emigrants rested and replenished supplies at Fort Bridger before crossing the last miles of present-day Wyoming land to the Bear River valley of Idaho. Travelers in 1993 did the same.

Earl Leggett:

EL Fort Laramie, it was good to get there, but it was also so windy, that it was sort of good to leave and get on down the road. Fort Bridger was completely different because it was a completely different place. At that point in time at Fort Bridger a lot of people were really getting tired. It was a well-needed stop to get ourselves together and prepared for that last hard push.

I had no health problems with Ann and Sue. I did have some collar sores, leather sores, from when we had all the rain, but never any colic problems. Mules adapt to feed probably better than a horse, they'll eat things a horse won't eat. My mules, in that BLM land we crossed near South Pass and western Wyoming, would stand in the sage, pull it up and eat it, a horse won't do that.

*Earl Leggett drives Sue and Ann past a trail marker in western Wyoming, not long after crossing South Pass. Following Earl is Phil Marincic of Pinedale, Wyoming.* (Candy Moulton Photo)

They did toughen up, they lost the fat, but turned into muscle. They weighed 1450 pounds when I bought them. I had to change from a size 21 collar to a size 20 collar with a pad under it at Fort Bridger, but that was because everything had just turned into muscle, I don't think their weight changed.

BEN KERN:

BK Aug. 2. We left Fort Bridger and came to Cumberland Flats. This is a bad camp. Greasewood, sagebrush.

BK Aug. 3. It thundered and lightninged and stormed. The old lightning was flashing all night long. We left Cumberland Flats for Kemmerer.

BK Aug. 4. From Kemmerer we took the Sublette Cutoff to Emigrant Springs. Muddy pulling the grade to Emigrant Springs. We didn't move camp, we left camp in Kemmerer, because it was so muddy the vehicles couldn't get there. So we came back to Kemmerer and camped here tonight.

As Hamilton Scott and his party neared western Wyoming in 1862, he again referred to the woman for whom his train delayed its start at Independence Rock:

HS ∩ July 27. We remained in camp all day. Thomas Paul's wife died about nine o'clock this morning. She died in childbirth. She has left behind an infant. She has been very poorly for some time. We buried her this evening under a large pine tree and put a post and paling fence around her grave. Our cattle stampeded last night about eleven o'clock. One hundred and fifty got away. We found them all but fifteen near. [A grizzly bear chased and stampeded the cattle.]

HS ∩ July 28. There were ten of the men started out this morning to hunt for the missing cattle. We hitched up at noon and drove ten miles, camping in the timber. No grass for stock. We have our cattle under yoke and chain them to trees. The men haven't come yet who went to look for the missing cattle.

HS ∩ August 2. Between eleven and twelve o'clock, our cattle scared at some loose horses belonging to another train. About twenty-five teams ran away, upsetting and breaking wagons, running over men, women and children. Mrs. Townsend from Monroe, Iowa was dangerously wounded. Wilson Scott had a broken leg. Mrs. Hoover's head was bruised....

HS ∩ August 3. Thomas Paul's child died last night and Mrs. Townsend, who was so seriously hurt in the stampede, died about twelve o'clock today. We buried them this evening.

There are many routes across western Wyoming which make up the Oregon, California, Mormon and Pony Express trail corridor. Of the four, the Pony Express had the shortest life, starting in April 1860 and running only eighteen months until October 1861. Organized by the freighting firm of Russell, Majors and Waddell, the Pony Express had five hundred horses, one hundred and ninety stations spaced about ten miles apart, and two hundred riders—mainly young orphan boys.

William F. Cody is one famous Pony Express rider. He once traveled 322 miles from Fort Laramie to Sweetwater Station and back, making the ride without rest because he found each station raided by Indians and abandoned by staff.

The service proved its worth in speed, but financially it failed. It died October 24, 1861, the day the transcontinental telegraph started operating. The telegraph lines also followed the trail corridor with offices at the former stage stops and at many of the Pony Express stations.

Indians hated the "talking wires" of the telegraph, perhaps because the lines symbolized the fact that the emigrants had come to stay rather than just to pass through the country. The Indians cut wires, burned poles, and raided stations in a vain attempt to get rid of the intruders.

BEN KERN:

BK Aug. 5. About an inch of snow on the ground this morning at Emigrant Springs. Left for Cokeville. I have a bad cold and am not feeling well. Real steep country. Had a lot of steep country, lot of muddy trail today. The steepest grade we've crossed on our journey. Real pretty through here, lots of wildflowers in bloom. Lots of grass. Got into Cokeville late this afternoon. Done about 18 miles today.

BK Aug. 6. We left Cokeville going toward the Bear River Divide. Crossed the Bear River and traveled the south side of the river. Camped tonight at the Bear River. Really steep climbs, a lot of steep hills.

CANDY MOULTON:

CM Behind are endless days of rain, hail, tornadoes, and even snow, plus for the modern travelers, miles of blacktop that wore out three sets of shoes on the horses, and three months of long, tiring days. Ahead are likely a lot more of the same.

Connie, Ray, and I sat outside, slapping mosquitoes the evening of August 5, as the sun fell behind the mountain. It lit the sagebrush with a rose-colored tint that faded to pale peach and then washed out altogether. As the moon rose, we gathered in the cook tent and ate cake to celebrate Marie's seventeenth birthday. Another cook quit, but a new one joined the train and will begin her duties tomorrow. This was the third or fourth cook to work and then quit while the wagons crossed Wyoming. It must have been a difficult job.

The morning of August 6 started out poorly. As we got ready to leave Cokeville, I realized I'd lost my billfold. It didn't have much in it: my driver's license, one credit card, and about forty dollars. I searched my car and the last campsite. I retraced my steps from the previous evening to no avail. I rummaged through my bags and found eleven dollars. That had to last me until I could get more money or get home. I knew I had only one more day with the train before I headed home and my car had a full tank of gas. Ben offered to give me ten dollars, but I declined. I thought how it was for the emigrants. They had what they had when they left Missouri. They lived from the land or made do without during the rest of their trip.

Elizabeth Stewart wrote in 1853: "Parted our company yesterday The Stevensons and Buckinghams took the old road and Loves and Stewards took the new one south."

The partings are so very difficult, even today as people leave new-found friends still headed west. Connie joined this train in mid-July when the train crossed her family's ranch near Ayres

Bridge. She planned to leave the train at Cokeville and arranged to catch a ride to Casper with Wyoming National Guardsmen who provided support for the train as it crossed Wyoming. They loaded her gear and headed down the road. The teams stood hitched to the wagons while Ben and Shawn put axle grease on some of the hubs. We were in our seats, ready to head out when the big green National Guard truck rolled back into camp. Connie said they were fifteen miles down the road before she told them to turn around so she could rejoin the train.

The overlanders left what is now Wyoming at the Smiths Fork crossing just northwest of present-day Cokeville. In 1843 John C. Frémont wrote the stream "is timbered with cottonwood, willow, and aspen and makes a beautiful debouchment through a pass about 600 yards wide, between remarkable mountain hills, rising abruptly on either side, and forming gigantic columns to the gate by which it enters the Bear river valley."

The Smiths Fork crossing and then the Thomas Creek crossing marked the emigrants' entry into Idaho.

In 1850 William Riley Franklin wrote:
WRF ∩ Camp 46. Thursday [July] 8th. We progressed about 10 miles. This brought us to Thomas Fork, which was considerably in our way as it was past fording. Therefore, resorted to this alternative, raised our wagon beds, carried ropes across to the opposite side and fastened them to our wagons and pulled them across, swam our mules, hitched up and advanced 8 miles farther and encamped where we found good water, wood and grass. Consequently, this night easily glided away.

WRF ∩ Camp 47. Friday 7th. We marched about 25 miles, crossing Bear River 4 times during our march. Here we found as good wild grass as grows in the world, consequently our mules lost no time, but ate greedily until they filled themselves.

During this day's march, we encountered two serious steep rocky and stupendous mountains to descend. In descending the last one we had to let our wagons down gradually with ropes. This, though is no difficulty and annoyance to what we met with from mosquitoes and their allies. When, where and how they chase on every side in small parties of 1000 in a squad, from their rear flank and front guard. Sometimes their whole army would sally forth from among some small sage path of 100 acres or out of some deep ravine or valley and annoy us, no little without receiving any material help. This, however, might be expected as we're traveling through Mosquito Nation.

Edwin Bird, in 1854 remarked on the mosquitoes in that area:
EB ∩ 1854. We first assended and descended a mountain when then passed over a roling road for about five miles when we came into Bear River Valley just before reaching the valley our road lay along a small spring brook which I shall take the liberty of calling frog crick it being literally alive with them. We then passed down Bear River to Smiths fork of the Same This is a pure cold mountain stream and abounds with trout. We camped early & close to the river here we found plenty of good grass for our Stock then most of us went fishing and caught some fine messes of trought to knight we had them for supper together with a can of Oysters which ws given to our men by a trader on Green River.... To knight we are camped in the great basin having passed over the last of the Rockey Mountains. We are also in the Banarx tribe of Indians Those are a well proportioned manly looking race. The soil is much richer here & the grass is plenty & good. Misquetoes are also troublesomly thick.

CANDY MOULTON:
CM I rode with Kris as we left Cokeville, trailing through town and then down a dirt road along the Bear River. As we

*"Yoking a Wild Bull" by William Henry Jackson. Oxen were the most commonly used draft animals on the Oregon Trail. They could pull greater loads than horses and did not require the daily ration of grain needed by horses. However, Jackson recorded that yoking the teams of oxen each morning could be quite an ordeal.* (Courtesy Scotts Bluff National Monument)

bounced over the rough dirt track, she drove and I read a gothic romance novel aloud to her. Shawn rode by and no doubt wondered what we were up to. Eventually he traded places with Kris. I put the book away as we headed up a steep hill: our climb over the Bear River Divide.

The long steady pull tired the horses, and some of them were showing the effects of the trip. Ben and Marie made it to the top without problems, but Connie, who drove Leeann's wagon, had Maggie and Molly give out on her a few hundred yards short of the crest. As the team faltered, Connie put all her weight against the brake rope, but the brake slipped off the wheel and the wagon rolled backwards, down the hill toward Jack and Mowitz, the team Shawn drove.

Dan, who was riding with Connie, quickly jumped from the wagon and shoved a rock behind the wheel. Shawn told me to get off his wagon to give the horses every chance to pull the hill. I stepped over the edge and jumped to the ground with my cameras in hand. Behind us Earl held steady with Ann and Sue. Ben walked down the hill, and he and Shawn decided the horses, Maggie and Molly, would need help to finish the climb. Rather than unhitching one of the teams already at the top, they had Lee back his four-wheel drive pickup to the wagon in trouble. They hitched the team and wagon to the truck with a chain.

With the added horsepower, the wagon easily went to the top of the hill. I took pictures of the pickup pulling the team and wagon to the top of the hill, but unfortunately somehow lost the film. Shawn drove his team over the divide and Earl followed. Neither had too much trouble. Dan and I walked. Once on top, we halted for lunch and let the teams rest for more than an hour. Another modern convenience crept into the day as we ate our lunch. Shawn pulled out his cellular telephone and made some phone calls to a radio station in Portland, Oregon, to see if they wanted to do an interview. I wondered if the irony of these compromises to modern technology bothered the other members of the train.

Earl Leggett:

EL All the wagons try to pace out when we go up a steep hill. You don't want to hold your animals back, you like to let them set their own pace. As we climbed out of Bear River, the teams in front of me quit. There was wagons all over the road and no place for me to go. We just sat there and waited. I think sometimes those bigger animals pulling all their gut weight tire out.... Their wagon weighed 2,000 pounds and they were on roller bearings. My wagon weighed 1,800 pounds, on the spindles that it was built with. Those bigger horses had all their weight to pull, too.

Candy Moulton:

CM Our afternoon had no steep climbs, but it was long and hot. We rolled up and down the back country road and didn't get to camp until nearly six P.M. Everyone was hot and tired. For supper the new cook made stew, fresh bread, and cake. The mosquitoes chewed hungrily.

Steep inclines into and out of the Thomas Fork of the Bear River gave overlanders their first taste of the land that is now Idaho. Although Oregon-bound travelers were more than halfway to their destination, they still had nearly a thousand miles to go. The hardships of the trail became more evident every day as the litter of abandoned and broken wagons marked its course.

The trail across Idaho was and is less visible because fewer travelers used it. Travelers headed to Oregon, California, and Mormons going to Utah used the route across Wyoming. But the Mormon travelers for the most part didn't enter Idaho. Instead they headed directly west toward Utah from Fort Bridger. As in Nebraska's Platte River valley, much of the trail in Idaho is plowed under and now in use as farm fields.

After crossing Thomas Fork, the first obstacle was a high ridge that became known as Big Hill. Then the pioneer wagons rolled to a trading post built and run in the late 1840s by Thomas L. "Peg Leg" Smith.

Mountain man Peg Leg Smith started his trading post in 1848 on the east bank of the Bear River. He took advantage of the Oregon-California trail traffic by selling supplies and services from his four log buildings. But the business had a short life of only about two years. Smith got his nickname—Peg Leg—because, as J. Goldsborough Bruff put it in 1849, "his leg was injured and he [got] out knife & amputated it himself, and afterward dressed [it], and fortunately recovered."

From Smith's trading post, the emigrants continued northwest along the Bear River passing a number of hot mineral springs before they reached the "soda" or "beer" springs, so called because the water had the taste of a natural soda or a slightly acidic beer.

William J. Scott on August 14, 1846, wrote of the area: "The Sody Spring is aquite acuriosity thare is agreat many of them Just boiling rite up out of the ground take alitle sugar an desolve it in alitle water and then dip up acup full and drink it before it looses it gass it is furstrate I drank ahol of galon of it you will see several Spring Spouting up out over the river."

The waters of Soda Point Reservoir today cover the springs. Even so it is sometimes possible to observe movement on the water surface caused by the springs. At Soda Springs, the Hudspeth Cutoff heads toward the southwest while the main Oregon Trail continued northwest until it joins the west end of the Lander Road, the cutoff which started from Western Wyoming.

Benoni M. Hudspeth first took the cutoff that bears his name as a part of the stampede to California in 1849.

**Ben Kern:**

BK Aug. 7. Left the camp at Bear River and headed over a steep hill. It was really a steep hill and we could only go a short distance before we had to let the horses take a breather. We started early this morning and the horses were fresh, but it took a long time to pull the hill this morning.

When we got to the top and started down into Montpelier we ran into Mormon crickets. They were so thick on the road that the horses kept shying and spooking from the crickets on the road. They'd crunch when the horses stepped on them. The

Mormon Crickets were about an inch and a half long and almost black. When the horses stepped on them, they squished and squashed. Mormon crickets got their common name after they descended on and nearly devoured Mormon crops in the Salt Lake valley the first year Mormons planted.

From the bottom of the big hill, to Montpelier the land is in a government set-aside program and isn't in production. It is all growed up with crested wheat and other grasses. The farmers don't do any harvest because the government pays them not to, like in Kansas. The crickets really congregated in this area.

Montpelier has a big celebration here at the top of the hill every year, to celebrate the Oregon Trail and other area history like the mountain men with a rendezvous. I attended the celebration a couple of years ago and they had a big cookout with a big trench and in it they had food cooking in 65 dutch ovens. In Montpelier we are staying at the fairgrounds.

Mormon crickets are native to the area, and many early travelers remarked about them including Harriet Talcott Buckingham, who wrote in 1851:

HTB 1851. The Crickets are large often an inch and a half or two inches in length—Black & shiney, the Indians make soup of them—They catch them by driving them into pits dug for this purpose—they are dried for winter use, it's laughable to see our White Chickens try to swallow them, it often takes two or three efforts to get one disposed of, they are so numerous that one cannot avoid stepping on them.

BEN KERN:

BK August 8-9. Laid over two days. Mark got real sick. I am afraid we won't be able to work him. The vet gave him some shots and tonight I walked him around. He ate good, drank, he just got better. This is the first time my horses got sick. Called the vet to give him some shots. It straightened him right up, I went ahead and worked with him. He is sick because we changed so many different river drainages. The vet told me the change of water affects the animals.

We went to the local Restaurant and Bar. We went up there and had a drink. There was a couple of guys in there, they had pool tables in the back. A couple of them were pool sharks and they'd been drinking pretty heavy. They were challenging some of the wagon train guys. These guys wanted us to put up money to play pool.

One of them was getting just plumb out of line. About the third or fourth time he come back and he was starting to give the wagon train guys a bad time. I got him by his shirt and I jumped off my stool. I pushed him over against the wall and told him, "Those guys don't want to play with you, now by God, leave us alone."

Bobby and I had a few more drinks. When we got ready to leave I said to him, "You're not gonna drive and I'm not gonna drive" and he said, "How're we gonna get home?" And I said "We're gonna walk." I just took off as fast as I could go. It was a couple miles back to the camp and he had a hard time keeping up with me.

BK Aug. 10. Left Montpelier and came to Georgetown. We heard about a mule for sale. We have been looking for mules all along the route.

BK Aug. 11. Came to Soda Springs. Shawn went back and bought Dunny, a nice zebra dun mule. Ticky Tack died here. When we were in Georgetown late last evening I fed the horses and I told Shawn there is something the matter with Ticky Tack. I told him, "You ought to call the vet, she's sick and not doing very good." I could see where she was really sick. Shawn told Erin or Marie to haul Ticky Tack to this campsite and if it looked like she is sick, then call a vet. They trailered her here to Soda Springs.

They got to Soda Springs and, as they unloaded her from the trailer, she just staggered over and fell over dead. Sometimes there isn't anything you can do to help an animal in a case like this. It reminded me of when Tom got colic in Nebraska and despite having a vet work on him, he died anyway.

A FAINT TRACE LEADS away from Soda Springs, not well-known by local residents, and certainly seldom viewed by visitors. One of the trail ruts crosses the Soda Springs Country Club west of town. The story goes that planners discovered the ruts as they prepared to build the country club. They laid out the golf course with the original trail swale as a part of the rolling terrain. Now about one thousand feet of Oregon Trail ruts cross through the greens and fairways of the golf course.

Also at Soda Springs is the burial site of a family killed in 1861, in what local legend calls a "massacre." They died at Little Spring Creek, a mile east of the marker in the Soda Springs Cemetery that now commemorates their lives and deaths. Trappers and other emigrants buried the parents and their five children in their own wagon box. Trail historians recognize their final resting place as the Wagon Box Grave, although they have no conclusive information about the deaths of the family.

BEN KERN:

BK Aug. 12. Left Soda Springs for Chesterfield. I'd been here the first part of March, when there was two foot of snow on the ground. This old boy had Belgian horses and he was feeding with a team and sled. Now in August we camped on his place, up the creek in a big grove of trees. A real pretty place to camp, a creek comes down through here. We had a really severe

*Watering the horses and mules at Big Springs, Idaho.* (Ben Kern Photo)

storm in the night. It thundered and lightninged and it raised hell all night long. It spooked the stock.

BK Aug. 13. We left Chesterfield for Big Springs. The support crew had a real hard time getting out of camp this morning because the two-track road was muddy and slick. Some of them had to drive through the meadow to get out. We came on the Fort Hall Shoshone-Bannock Reservation. This morning we went by Chesterfield Lake which is a real big lake on the reservation. There was lots of people fishing the lake, boats and campers everyplace. Big Springs is a real pretty place, lots of willows and lots of grass, a species I know as Timothy, the Timothy is two feet high.

BK Aug. 14. We left Big Springs for Ketchel Meadows. The first day we were on the Indian reservation, the rider for the Indians who took care of the cattle joined us. They have about 3,000 head of cattle on the south side of the reservation.

When we got to Ketchel Meadows, the Indian rider was with us. They also run about 3,000 head of cattle on the north side of the reservation.

We turned the horses loose in a big meadow. We kept two wrangle horses in the corrals the Indian rider has at his camp here. We can use those horses to get our teams in when we need them. We laid over a day and I washed clothes in the creek. I gathered all my clothes and I got one of the plastic chairs we had in camp, and I went to the creek and I washed my clothes and I set the chair in the creek and I sat in it and I was taking a sun bath. I had that chair sitting in a deep hole in the water. I was way back in the willows and I thought I was hid, some gal snuck up behind me and took my picture.

THE NEXT STOP on the route was Fort Hall, which served as the third of the three major provisioning places for emigrants.

BEN KERN:

BK Aug. 15. We came from Ketchel Meadows to Fort Hall. The road brought us over some real steep places and we had to make some real sharp turns to go around cattleguards in fences. In one spot the bolster—which sets on top of the running gears and holds the wagon box in place—on one wagon shifted. The wagon box slid to the side and started rubbing on the wagon wheels. We had to stop and get all hands together to move the box. We had to pick up the box—using the brake rods from all the wagons as pry bars—in order to reposition the bolster. Then we put the bed back where it belonged. It took us about an hour to get the wagon back into operation. When we got to Fort Hall we laid over a day. We were there during their Indian celebration. They had all their Indian dances.

The day we laid over the man who is in charge of the buffalo pasture and all the buffalo on the Fort Hall Reservation took

*All hands help reposition the wagon box on one of the Conestogas after the bolster shifted and caused the box to rub on the wagon wheel.* (Ben Kern Photo)

Shawn and I out through the buffalo pasture. They call it the Big Bottoms, and they have about 500 head of wild horses. We seen a lot of the horses. He drove us around the reservation and we looked at the big springs.

This is pretty country. Lots of beaver dams, quaker groves, and lots of fish in the ponds. He told us a lot of the history. Old Fort Hall, where they had the original Fort Hall was on the Snake River. He took us down and showed us where the original site was. They're trying to re-establish that and put it back where the old original fort was.

THE TENSION ESCALATED on the 1993 train as it crossed eastern Idaho, with several people, including Connie, leaving the party by the time the train reached Fort Hall and Pocatello.

Earl put the situation into this perspective:

EL I tried myself to get up every morning and tell myself that I had a goal. Ben and I, we had a job to do and every morning I would get up and get on down the road and do what we needed to do at night and try not to be part of any dissension. It was an existence. You had to have a strong will some days that we were out there. You had to be tough to go ahead and will yourself to make it through that day and the next day.

[The tension] came from a lot of people being away [from home] for a long time, being tired.

Sometimes we'd just sit and talk by ourselves and get away from what else was going on. I think we, Ben and I, do that because we have respect for one another. We sort of have a pact that no matter what happens, we are going to finish the trip. He has a goal and I have a goal, it was to leave Independence and come through and somehow or another we are going to do it.

FORT HALL GOT its start as a stockaded trading post built by Nathaniel J. Wyeth in 1834 on the east bank of the Snake River between the mouth of the Portneuf and Bannock Rivers. In 1837 the fort sold to the British Hudson Bay Company and a year later it was rebuilt by covering the log stockade with adobe bricks. Although originally used as a fur trader and trapper supply point, after 1849, the Hudson Bay Company managed the fort for the benefit of emigrants headed to Oregon and California. Fort Hall remained in use until its abandonment in 1856 due to increasing difficulties with the Indians of the region.

Historians don't agree on the precise location of the original Fort Hall, but it sat near present-day Pocatello in an area with a slough on the east side and a bank of willow and cottonwood trees on the west side. Most agree the Oregon Trail passed just west of the fort. The fort site is on the Fort Hall Indian Reservation and is managed by the Shoshone-Bannock Tribal Council. It currently serves as a grazing area for tribal livestock and is an unofficial wildlife refuge.

BEN KERN:

BK Aug. 16. We left Fort Hall to go to Pocatello. When we left, we took the wagons and went right through the buffalo pasture. We went through two different herds of buffalo. We had buffalo on both sides of us. The horses really paid attention, but didn't spook. We stayed at the fairgrounds at Pocatello. This is about the quietest place we have stayed. We have access to everything. There wasn't a soul that came out. There wasn't nobody here. We laid over two days at Pocatello.

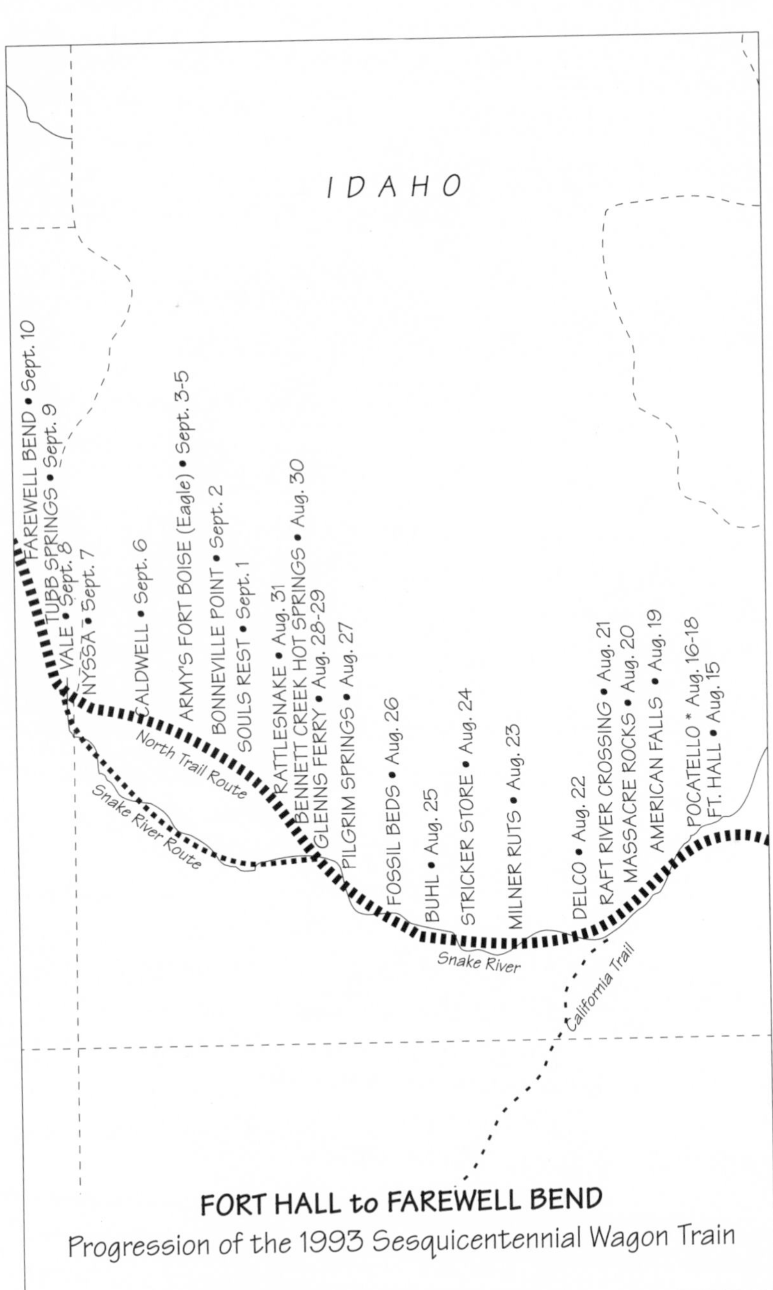


**FORT HALL to FAREWELL BEND**

Progression of the 1993 Sesquicentennial Wagon Train

PART SEVEN:

# *Fort Hall to Farewell Bend*

*"Watch that balloon, it'll scare my mules."*
—Earl Leggett, 1993

Fort Hall, Idaho. Goodale's Cutoff left Fort Hall heading north and then turned west past what is now Craters of the Moon National Monument. That cutoff went through Boise and on to the Payette and Weiser River country before heading north into Oregon. The Goodale Cutoff became particularly popular after miners discovered gold in northern Idaho in 1862.

Tim Goodale pioneered the route when he steered wagons north of Massacre Rocks on the main branch of the Oregon Trail. Nathan Hall, founder of Fort Hall, also used the route as a supply line to the mouth of the Columbia River. Nathaniel Wyeth made the first documented crossing on the route in 1834. It is now embraced by the Idaho National Engineering Laboratory. Ben Kern traveled the Goodale Cutoff in 1994 and his journal is included in the appendix of this volume.

The main Oregon Trail, which Ben and the sesquicentennial wagon train followed in 1993, left Fort Hall and headed west along the Snake River.

Ben Kern:

BK Aug. 19, 1993. We left Pocatello to go to American

Falls. We stayed at the fairgrounds and they are just getting ready to have their rodeo.

BK Aug. 20. We left American Falls to go to Massacre Rocks. Today we were having lunch and we were way out from nowhere when a Schwann's ice cream truck came by and the driver bought us an ice cream bar. We have a real pretty campsite at Massacre Rocks, on the park lawn amongst the trees. We turned the horses loose in a fenced in place across the road from Massacre Rocks and they had access to a creek that runs down through here. All the horses got in the creek and played in the water. The horses just pawed that water, some of them laid down and rolled. They just had a ball. I pulled my pickup over in the pasture tonight to sleep and stay where the horses are.

*The trail from Missouri to Oregon was long, but these five wagons made the entire trip.* (Bill White Photo)

BK Aug. 21. It was Kris's turn to get up and help me feed the horses. It rained in the night, just sprinkled a little bit. I woke up real early to look at my watch and it was about 4 o'clock. I seen a lantern coming from the camp across the road. It was Kris's, she rattled on my window and said, "Come on get up, it's time to feed the horses." I said, "Kris it's only four o'clock, for God's sake, go back to bed." She did and never did get up to help this morning.

We left Massacre Rocks to go to Raft River. This is a sad day. We'd been using a pickup and horse trailer that belonged to Stan Vogel and today Eric left to take them and go back home. He said he won't come back. We all hated to see him leave. Eric had been with us since Independence. When he left the girls were all crying. I'm trying to keep from crying. We camped on the Lyle Woodbury ranch.

When we were planning this trip before we left Casper, a woman at the meeting had a diary of the Henry Hayes family. When I went to Raft River to visit Woodbury to get permission to camp, the rancher told me about a little gravesite. He said he's going to build a bridge to it. I asked if there were any names, and he said yes, one was "Henry Hayes." In this diary the woman wrote a poem for every day. She wrote, "Today we left Raft River and I left my husband Henry behind."

At American Falls the emigrants marveled at the power of the then free-flowing Snake River.

"We passed the great American falls. The fall must be 40 to 50 feet in about 70 or 80 yards.... The roaring of the waters can be heard for many miles. They rush with great velocity over and through the vast lumps that lay in massive piles in the channel," James A. Pritchard wrote July 5, 1849.

Just southwest of American Falls, Indians and overlanders tangled in a skirmish that left ten emigrants dead. The fight occurred in a rocky outcropping on August 9 and 10, 1862. While the wagon train of Hamilton Scott rested for noon they heard that Indians and travelers on another wagon train were involved in a conflict.

The Scott party went to help the other travelers, but found one emigrant dead, two others wounded, and several missing. The teams used for pulling the wagons had disappeared. The rescuers towed the wagons to the rocky outcrop only to find that another train also had been fighting Indians. Sources are conflicting, but in all five to ten emigrants died. The three trains then joined together to continue their western journey.

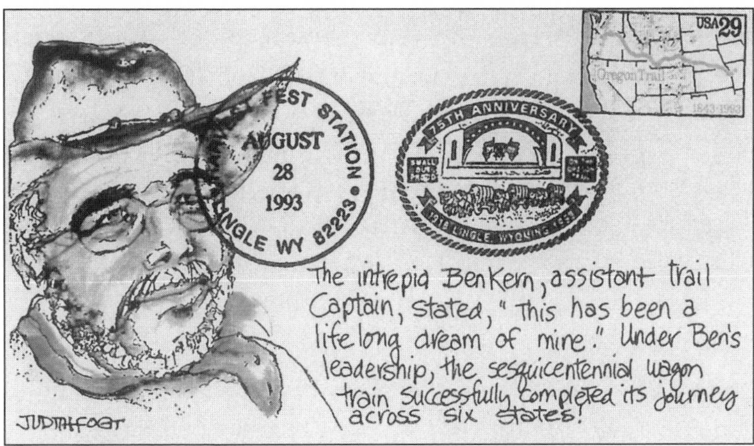


*Postal commemorative cachet of Ben Kern.* (Judith Fogt)

*Postal commemorative of Earl Leggett.* (Judith Fogt)

The site of the fighting is now a state park.

BEN KERN:

BK Aug. 22. We left Raft River to go to Delco, we drove our wagons right by the gravesite where Henry Hayes is buried, then we pulled a real steep hill and when we got to the top of the hill, that's where the California Trail took off and we followed it today. We went about eight miles down the California Trail. We got into Delco and we stayed at the rodeo grounds. Several people came out and brought us homemade bread, cakes, pies, cookies. They hauled a lot of stuff out.

One lady came and asked us if we wanted some homemade bread. We said yes and she said she'd go home and bake it. About 7 o'clock her husband came and said the bread wasn't done, but not to go to bed until she brings it. About 10 o'clock here she comes with about eight loaves of homemade bread and fresh butter she had churned. Here we are at 10 o'clock eating homemade bread and butter.

South Central Idaho became another "parting of the ways" for the emigrants. There they had to decide whether to continue west to the verdant Oregon country or to head southwest on the California Trail.

About fourteen miles west of Massacre Rocks, the trails to Oregon and California diverge for the final time. The split comes just after the route crosses the Raft River, with a left fork headed southwest toward California and a right trace turning northwest to Oregon. While those seeking their fortunes in the gold fields after the 1849 rush to California did take that trail, many emigrants continued on toward Oregon.

Other trails split off before this point: major cutoffs were the Salt Lake Route, which left at Fort Bridger; the Hudspeth Cutoff, which left at Sheep Rock; and the Goodale Cutoff, which parted at Fort Hall. Raft River was the time of final decision making. Although the Forty-Niners knew they wanted to head toward the gold diggings, a surprising number of emigrants didn't make a decision until they watched the water drip from their wagon wheels after fording Raft River.

This, then, is the final parting of the ways on the Oregon

and California Trails. Three distinct rut lines mark the hill. The decision point itself is in the middle of a flat field surrounded by grass and sage.

**Ben Kern:**

BK Aug. 23. We left Delco and our next campsite is Milner Ruts. Milner Ruts is a state park, right on the Snake River. We camped right on the Snake River. Mosquitoes are horrible. The horses tore the picket line down a couple of times fighting the mosquitoes and flies. In all of our trip, this was the biggest feed that we had so far. People from all of the community came out. They had barbequed ribs. They brought cantaloupe, watermelon, tomatoes. One lady made fried squaw bread. We had to start some smudge pots tonight in a tent to keep the mosquitoes out.

BK Aug. 24. We left Milner Ruts for Stricker Store. Stricker Store has a lot of history. It got its name because there used to be a big family name of Stricker Brothers. They had a big ranch and run a lot of cattle. This was their headquarters and it was the stage stop, too. The old stage house, the old log barns, and the old cellar are still here where they kept their supplies. They used to sell whiskey here and kept whiskey in the cellar. The old stage house and everything is really in good shape. Everything is still intact.

BK Aug. 25. We went from Stricker Store to Buhl at the fairgrounds. Not much happened today.

Emigrants camped along Rock Creek long before the first trading post established on the Oregon Trail west of Fort Hall opened in the area. Stricker Store was built in 1863, making the camping site even more popular. The store later served as Rock Creek Station, a stop on the Ben Holladay stage line, and is the only original stage station remaining from that line which connected Utah and Idaho during pre-railroad days.

*"Three Island Crossing" by William Henry Jackson. Near present-day Glenns Ferry, Idaho, this site allowed the teamsters to cross the treacherous Snake River by using three islands as 'stepping stones.'* (Courtesy Scotts Bluff National Monument)

Many of the original buildings remain, including the sod-roofed Stricker Store, and they are in private ownership. West of the store, along the Rock Creek bank, the ruts of the Oregon Trail are clear, and so is the site of the emigrant campground.

Overlanders paralleled the south bank of the Snake River passing the magnificent Shoshone Falls, which originally had the name Canadian Falls. Higher than Niagara Falls, at 212 feet, historic travelers could hear the roar and splash of the water as far away as five miles.

The emigrants often didn't even see the falls, however, because they feared straying from the trail—which had good grazing and water—since in later years there were some problems with Indians who resented the steady encroachment into their territory.

"Could easily hear the sound of a waterfall," Osborne Cross wrote August 15, 1849. "Much surprised to learn the next day that within ten miles of this place there is a cascade which is not surpassed by the Niagara falls."

**Ben Kern:**

BK Aug. 26. We got to Fossil Beds. We stayed at a trailer park and swimming pool. We camped up on a hill in a part of the park. They brought in sweet corn. They cooked a whole gob of sweet corn and had a big feed with a lot of fruit.

BK Aug. 27. We left Fossil Beds and went to Pilgrim Springs. Pilgrim Springs is really an isolated place. It is used as a beet dump where they dump their sugar beets in the fall. It is really isolated. There isn't nothing around here.

BK Aug. 28. Left Pilgrim Springs for Glenns Ferry. At Glenns Ferry we stayed at the Three Island Park on the river. We stayed right where they re-enact the Three Island crossing every year. Last year they lost some wagons and drowned a horse or two during the re-creation and some old-timers said they aren't going to do it any more. They put in a ferry, but the power company would only let them have the cable there for so long, so the ferry isn't running and we didn't get to cross the river on the ferry there. We followed a road across the bridge instead. We had arrangements to stay at the fairgrounds, but there was a change in personnel and the new lady had leased out the land. So we went and talked with the manager at Three Island Park. He gave us permission to camp. We have a real nice campsite. We laid over a day. Quite a bunch of us went to the winery and some gals who were riding the train took us to test the wine and we had supper. The vineyard was right out in back. The restaurant is on the second floor, all glassed in and you can look out over the vineyard.

Near what is now Glenns Ferry, emigrants had to make a difficult choice. They could cross the deep, dangerous Three Island Crossing of the Snake or stay on the dry, rough south alternate route of the Oregon Trail.

An estimated half of the emigrants did attempt the treacherous crossing, considered the most important and most difficult river crossing in Idaho. Many lost their possessions, others their lives and livestock. On October 3, 1843, John C. Frémont, as he scouted the western trail, crossed at Three Island.

He wrote:

JCF ∩ 1843. About 2 o'clock we arrived at the ford where the road crosses to the right bank of the Snake River. An Indian was hired to conduct us through the ford, which proved impracticable for us, the water sweeping away the howitzer and nearly drowning the mules, which we were obliged to extricate by cutting them out of the harness. The river here is expanded into a little bay, in which there are two islands, across which is the road of the ford; and the emigrants had passed by placing two of their heavy wagons abreast of each other, so as to oppose a considerable mass against the body of water.

On August 14, 1845, Samuel Parker wrote of the crossing, "To Snake River—crossed very deep to hind wheels—7 yoke to a wagon."

The crossing could be deadly, but so could the alternative—staying on the south side of the river and following a dry trail that passed through what are today called the Bruneau Sand Dunes.

The islands themselves appear to have changed little in the past century and a half, if early drawings are a realistic portrayal of the way it was. The country around the crossing, however, is now turned to the plow and one of Idaho's agricultural centers.

Ben Kern:

BK Aug. 30. We left Glenns Ferry and went to Bennett Creek Hot Springs. It used to be a real big hot springs, but over the years it just quit. The springs quit working. There wasn't no more hot springs.

One 1843 emigrant journal said the Hot Springs, which formed the head of Hot Springs Creek, were hot enough to "cook an egg." John C. Frémont put the temperature of the springs at 164 degrees Fahrenheit that same year. They became a favored emigrant camping spot. In later years an entrepreneur built a stone spring house and promoted the area as a spa.

Today the springs don't smoke and foam any longer. In fact they don't have any water at all because of a lower water table caused by irrigation and water supply demands.

The main branch of the Oregon Trail headed north after Three Island Crossing to meet the Boise River and Fort Boise, a trading post the Hudson Bay Fur Company established in 1834. Like Fort Hall, the original wood structure eventually had an adobe covering. Flood waters in 1853 severely damaged Fort Boise. The Hudson Bay post should not be confused with the Fort Boise established by the army in 1863 as a cavalry post to protect gold miners and Oregon Trail travelers. The army's Fort Boise sat nearly fifty miles east of the Hudson Bay post at a site now in the city of Boise, Idaho.

Ben Kern:

BK Aug. 31. We left Bennett Creek headed for Rattlesnake camp. We stayed on the Steve Percy ranch. We're traveling on the north side of the Snake River now. A very hot and dry camp. We stayed in a stackyard where a guy stacked his hay. It is rocky and dry and dusty. He had a set of corrals and he had it all set up and he had water, but they're redoing the highway. One of the ditch diggers came in and as he did he cut the water line. This rancher had a water truck and we filled it up over by his ranch buildings, so we had water.

BK Sept. 1. We left Rattlesnake going to Souls Rest camp. This area is where the Goodale Trail rejoins the Oregon Trail.

BK Sept. 2. We left Souls Rest going to Bonneville Point. This is rolling, hill country. There was an old stage station between Souls Rest and Bonneville Point that we passed today.

Earl's birthday is the fourth of September. His wife, Dorothy, had planned to join him for a while when the train reached Casper, but her mother had become ill and passed away and she was unable to come to Casper. Although they'd talked on the telephone, Earl and Dorothy hadn't seen each other for more than four months. As the train neared Boise, a surprise awaited Earl.

Earl Leggett:

EL We was downtown Boise at noon. I seen this person coming down the street and I thought I should know. She's carrying a balloon. Then I realized who it was. The first thing out of my mouth was "Watch that balloon, it'll scare my mules."

Ben Kern:

BK Sept. 3. We left Bonneville Point. This was a very very steep, rough trail. We came from Bonneville into Boise and it was really really rough. We left at 4 o'clock this morning because we had to be in front of the city hall in Boise at 11 o'clock. So we harnessed in the dark and left in the dark. We stopped in Boise at City Hall. The mayor had a nice dedication on the front steps. The mayor gave us the Idaho flag.

Earl's wife showed up. He didn't know she was coming. She had a whole bunch of balloons tied together. She was on the back side of city hall. We pulled up right in front of city hall. Earl saw this woman with the balloons and he was concerned that they would spook his mules. Pretty soon he said, "Jesus Christ, that's my wife." He didn't even know she was going to be here. We left Boise and came on to Eagle, Idaho, to camp.

We laid over here for a couple of days. In the morning I was getting ready to leave for town and I saw the truck from the Humane Society drive up to the gate, I got out to visit with the man in the truck and he said somebody had turned us in and he had to come out and investigate. I went back with him and we went out and looked at the horses. I showed him all of our type of feed and the mineral we were using. And he said, "I don't know why anybody turned you in, because I've never seen a better bunch of horses." He give us a good report that said he couldn't see anything wrong. The horses are in good shape.

As the trail neared Oregon, some emigrants on an alternate route used the Olds Ferry to cross the Snake River near what is now the town of Weiser where sand dunes and badlands resemble those near Scotts Bluff, Nebraska. The emigrants continued their march west. They had covered more than three-quarters of the journey and were ready to begin the last leg.

West of Bonneville Point, the emigrants had a reprieve from harsh conditions along the trail when they reached Fort Boise. Theodore Talbot on October 14, 1843, described the fort as "one of the smallest we have visited, is neatly constructed of Adobes and belongs to [Hudson] Bay Company."

James Field on August 23, 1845, wrote that the fort is "a small, mean-looking fort, built like other of sundried mud moulded into the shape of bricks, and appears more calculated for the collection of furs from other forts than for trading in its

*Ben Kern prepares a peach cobbler in his dutch oven.* (Ben Kern Photo)

own immediate vicinity, as there is no game there, and the Indians living in this part of the country are very poor, many of them nearly naked and living on fish and roots."

"Most of the country is a barren waste," Loren B. Hastings wrote September 22, 1847.

Although confrontations with various Indian tribes occurred all along the route of the Oregon Trail, for the most part they were minor incidents with the loss of only limited numbers on both sides. One of the greatest losses to the emigrants took place near Hudson Bay's Fort Boise August 20, 1854—at just about the same time as the Grattan fight near Fort Laramie.

The fight and the deaths of eighteen emigrants took place twenty-two miles east of the fort in a battle often referred to as the Ward Massacre. The emigrants were part of the Alexander Ward train, and only two young boys survived when the Indians left them for dead. Another emigrant party rescued one boy, and the other boy made his way to Fort Boise.

Military reprisal was severe. Unfortunately it didn't come with any measure of justice. The army hanged any Indians caught in the area. The tribes rose in defense, engaging in subsequent harsh and bloody battles. One consequence of the attack and military retribution was the abandonment of Forts Hall and Boise which resulted in extremely hazardous travel for emigrants for nearly a decade.

BEN KERN:

BK Sept. 6. We left Eagle on the way to Caldwell, Idaho. We stayed at the Simplot fairgrounds in Caldwell. A lot of my friends and a lot of my relations came and visited with us at the camp. During the night one of Marie's horses colicked so the girls stayed up all night.

BK Sept. 7. We left Caldwell and are headed for Nyssa, Oregon, our next camp. On the way, Jumbo, Erin's horse, colicked and we had load him up on the trailer. Shawn and Erin was taking him back to Caldwell to the vet and he died on the trailer before they got there. When horses colic their intestine ties up. If they get down, they get a twist in their gut and they don't ever get over it. A change causes colic. Feed is the big factor.

Merle Pfeiffer, he's my cousin, was at Caldwell to visit with me. He lives out of Parma and tomorrow we will go right by his place. Tonight at Vale, my Aunt Ethel and her daughter Marion and her husband Roger came to see me. I was out on the trail, checking where we will go tomorrow. I drive ahead on the trail nearly every night to be sure of the route. When my relatives arrived, the first person they run into was Earl and they asked him if I was around. He asked if they were relations and my Aunt Ethel said she's my Aunt. Earl replied, "God damn he's got relation under every bush." My Aunt Ethel is 91 and she just blows and goes.

We had a big reception at Nyssa. When we entered Nyssa a big crowd greeted us. This lady Earl knows real well, head of the Aurora Chamber of Commerce, gave us the Oregon flag. The Oregon governor intended to be here, but couldn't come because of a family illness.

Overlanders reached the country then called Oregon at South Pass in present-day Wyoming, but their destination was much farther west in the Willamette valley.

Emigrants started their final crossing of what is now the state of Oregon at the Snake River Crossing near Nyssa. Then they crossed Keeney Pass west along the Snake River in a dry and dusty trek across an alkali desert. They had difficult traveling with few opportunities to replenish supplies. The Indians who lived along the route were vitally important, particularly in the early years, as they traded with weary travelers.

July 15, 1852, Lydia Allen Rudd, with her family in Wyoming wrote, "Some of the snake indians came to our camp this morning I swaped some hard bread with them for some good berries." A month later in Idaho she wrote, "bought a salmon fish of an indian today weighing seven or eight pounds gave him an old shirt some bread and a sewing needle."

Ben Kern:

BK Sept. 8. We left Nyssa enroute to Vale, Oregon. At Nyssa we crossed the river to the south side. We went the original ruts from Nyssa to Vale.

As we approached my cousin Merle's place I could see him standing there waiting for us. He had a bushel basket full of tomatoes, and cantaloupe, watermelon and onions. He was standing out alongside the road waiting to put it on the wagon.

Went over Keeny Pass, where there is a big monument. This was on the old original Oregon Trail. We stayed at the fairgrounds/rodeo grounds in Vale. A lot of people came out tonight and they gave us a feed.

BK Sept. 9. My birthday and I can't even celebrate. We came to Tubb Springs. This is a bad camp. There is no water. Sandburrs, weeds, dust. It is really bad.

BK Sept. 10. Kris stayed up all night and baked me a cake. She baked a three layer cake. She put coloring in the cake batter so each layer was a different color. She done this in the old cook trailer. Three o'clock in the morning here she came, got me up and said, "You gotta come over here and look at something." So I got up. Looked at the cake then we put it in the freezer.

We left Tubb Springs for Farewell Bend. We went out across Mormon Basin. It was really bad. Dusty, dirty, dry. We got into Farewell Bend. We camped at Farewell Bend State Park. We have a nice campsite here. Tonight the people of the town of Huntington invited us all to come over and have supper, which is about six miles from Farewell Bend. My aunt, all of my cousins, all of my relation was here, and they really put on a feed. We had a big party. I think I wound up with about five cakes. They really put on a big feed here, they had all kinds of stuff. A railroad park with engines and stuff. This is where I celebrated my birthday.

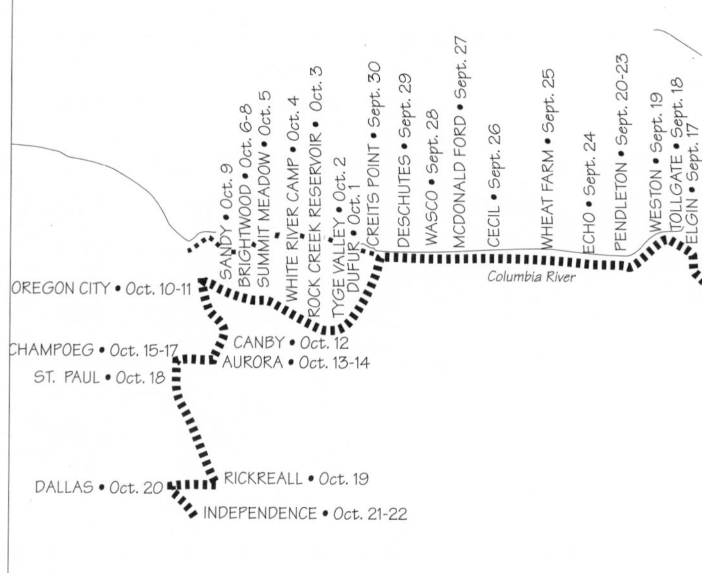


**FAREWELL BEND to INDEPENDENCE**

Progression of the 1993 Sesquicentennial Wagon Train

PART EIGHT:

# Farewell Bend to Independence, Oregon

*"It's friendships like this that you build across the whole trail that you couldn't buy."*

—Earl Leggett, 1993

At Farewell Bend, the emigrants said goodbye to the Snake River, after following its course for 350 miles. They went up Burnt River Canyon and through the pass below Flagstaff Hill. Before them loomed the Blue Mountains.

"In passing across the mountains we were overtaken by a snow storm which made the prospect very dismal. I remember wading through mud and snow and suffering from the cold and wet," Jesse Applegate wrote as he and his family crossed the Blue Mountains in 1843.

Ben Kern:

BK Sept. 11. We left Farewell Bend to Weatherby State Park. A pretty campsite. The same people from Huntington came to Weatherby and cooked our supper again and they had a fish fry. Had fried bread and had two kegs of beer, lots of whiskey to drink. I celebrated my birthday again. At Farewell Bend we saw the Snake for the last time.

BK Sept. 12. We left Weatherby State Park, headed for Pleasant Valley. Quiet camp, not many people came out. We cooked our own supper. Big hills. From Weatherby we went north then crossed the interstate [highway] and finally traveled on the south side of the interstate.

EARL LEGGETT:

EL Probably the most memorable experience of the whole journey was…the people you make friends with, they kept you going day to day. The trip was getting hard and long and we came into Idaho and western Idaho and eastern Oregon. After four to five months you're getting tired and you need some new strength, somebody familiar you can talk with, somebody you know.

Ben Kern became a very good friend of mine. He drove the lead wagon across the trail. He was a cowboy, he was a logger, he'd done a little of everything. The girls called him Gentle Ben. He was a stabilizing factor, he never got excited.

Times along the trail Ben and I would talk and sometimes we'd…just go off and sorta get lost. It's friendships like this that you build across the whole trail that you couldn't buy.

SOME FORTY-EIGHT miles northwest of Farewell Bend, emigrants crossed Flagstaff Hill, the summit of which was reached only after a long, hard pull up through Virtue Flat. At the peak, travelers saw before them a downhill grade, and even more important, in the distance they saw the Blue Mountains, made that color by the growth of yellow pine trees.

Seeing trees in such density became a definite landmark for the emigrants who'd seen few since starting their trip. Trees are scarce to almost nonexistent all along the route from Kansas and Nebraska through Wyoming and Idaho. Finally in Oregon, that land of the chosen, trees covered the landscape.

BEN KERN:

BK Sept. 13. Left Pleasant Valley for Baker City. My mom

and step dad came out today and rode back into Baker with us. We stayed at the fairgrounds in Baker. We had a real big celebration tonight. Maybe 100 people or better from Grant County where I used to live came over to see me. We had a ceremony and supper in the 4-H building at the fairgrounds.

BK Sept. 14. We left Baker City for North Powder. We got in early today, only had 15 miles to go. Stayed at the fairgrounds. The committee furnished all the hay for our horses and they put on a feed for us here.

BK Sept. 15. We left North Powder and went to Union. Stayed at the fairgrounds. They had hay for the horses and also gave us feed.

BK Sept. 16. Left Union to head to Elgin, we camped on a rancher's place the first night out of Union. This wasn't on the Oregon Trail, but there was a wagon trail that went up through here. We camped on a hill. This house on the ranch is a two story house with a cupola on top. The reason for it is that this was a toll road and they had a guy stay up there all day long and watch for the wagons.

BK Sept. 17. We left the ranch campsite and went on to Elgin. Stayed at the fairgrounds. Big feed.

FROM THE TOP OF Flagstaff Hill, the trail winds down through the Ladd Canyon and across the wide Grande Ronde valley. This is fertile country—then and now—and it might have been tempting to some emigrants to settle here. But the pioneers had a farther goal in mind and very few broke away early to stop their trek before they got to the Willamette valley. After traversing the Grand Ronde valley, the emigrants entered the Blue Mountains, the first forest terrain encountered since eastern Kansas.

Some early travelers stood at South Pass and, knowing they'd crossed the backbone of the country, assumed the rest of their trip would be easy. They soon found that the mountains of Oregon presented quite a challenge. While climbing the Blues, the trail became rougher as it wound up and through the forest.

The shade provided some relief from high temperatures. A definite advantage to traveling through and over the Blue Mountains was the ready availability of wood and water. The Blues were a major landmark and the beginning of a tough trail across the timbered Pacific Northwest.

The forest canopy of the Blue Mountains shelters the Oregon Trail ruts, and they are in good shape as they wind over the hills. The greatest threat to the trail in this area is logging development, particularly on private lands, which the trail crosses.

North of Meacham is the site of Emigrant Springs, used as a routine stopping place after being discovered in 1834 by Jason Lee, an Oregon-bound missionary. The springs provided water for emigrants, but they are no longer in existence, having been destroyed by pipeline and highway construction during the twentieth century.

Not all of the emigrants traveled all the way to the Willamette valley. Some stopped at earlier choice spots, as did Hamilton Scott in 1862. In eastern Oregon he wrote:

HS ∩ September 13. Drove eight miles, camped on Burnt River at noon. Captain Kennedy resigned this morning and the company is well pleased because he did. He and his men that he furnished with teams camped by themselves this evening. We understand that we have been in Oregon for forty-five miles but we are sixty-five miles from settlement yet. The first settlement is on Powder River. They are gold miners.

HS September 14. Drove ten miles up Burnt River. There is some birch and cotton wood on this stream. The first we have seen excepting some willows since we left the Bear Mountains. Our principal fuel was sagebrush and willows.

HS September 15. Drove twelve miles, camped still on the same stream. There were high mountains on both sides of us. We have twenty-one in our company. We have elected Mr. Hall as our Captain.

HS September 17. Drove fourteen miles, camped at a spring but no water for our stock.

HS September 18. Five miles brought us to where the roads part, one leading to Fort Walla Walla and the other to Powder River gold mines at Auburn, Oregon. I, with a number of others, took the latter road. Camped on Powder River ten miles from Auburn.

BEN KERN:

BK Sept. 18. Left Elgin for Tollgate. Tollgate is the very summit of the Blue Mountains. We are on top of the Blue Mountains. I wanted to go the original route to LaGrande and Spring Creek, and Emigrant Springs, down Deadman Pass off the hill into Mission, and into Pendleton. We didn't get to go that away, instead we came toward Milton-Freewater. It was really really cold. Got down and frosted. Stayed at a little store, restaurant, and bar. Out in back the owner had a big fireplace with a huge gazebo. He had about 20 cord of wood, so we kept the fires agoing. We cooked on the fireplace. We really enjoyed that.

BK Sept. 19. Left Tollgate for Milton-Freewater. Have a very very poor noon campsite, not hardly room enough to camp. This was supposed to be a big celebration for us, but it didn't pan out. Later we camped at Weston on a ranch. A nice campsite. We circled the wagons right in the rancher's yard. He had a nice set of corrals that we put our horses in.

BK Sept. 20. The lady at the restaurant in Weston had us down for breakfast. We had a lame horse so Shawn decided we'd work Dunny, the mule we bought in Idaho. We put the harness on him and put a set of Running Ws on him. This is the same kind of set-up I used on Tom when we left Topeka and he and Jerry wanted to run away. If the mule decided to run, Shawn could pull the line and force him to slow down. Shawn and Erin drove him and Jerry together today. It was quite a show, Dunny just throwed a fit all day long, he never would settle down and work. We got into Pendleton. Where we came over the Blues was rougher and steeper than if we'd have followed the original route. From Elgin to Tollgate it is pull all the way. It is steep and on pavement so there was a lot more traffic. The original route would have been on less traveled roads.

In Pendleton we are at the Roundup grounds. We camped right in the middle of the Indian encampment where all of the Indians camp during the Pendleton Roundup. Laid over in Pendleton three days.

SOUTHEAST OF present-day Pendleton, historic wagon trains went through a narrow pass between Buckaroo and Deadman Pass creeks.

The pass didn't get the appellation Deadman until after the Oregon emigration. At least three separate instances involving violent death occurred in the area. It is most likely the name came from an incident during the Bannock War of 1878 when Indians killed seven men in three different attacks.

The Oregon Trail travelers found Deadman Pass an important landmark. It put them over the Blue Mountains and into the Umatilla valley. They had only two hundred miles to go before reaching their destination. From certain locations at the north end of Deadman Pass, visitors can see the Oregon trace as it falls into the Umatilla valley. Ruts remain on Emigrant Hill, and at the bottom is a junction with the route that provided access to and from the Whitman Mission.

The earliest people to emigrate to Oregon in 1843 and 1844 went by way of the Whitman Mission east of Walla Walla, Washington, but later travelers only went there if they needed food, medicine or other help.

Marcus and Narcissa Whitman established their mission among the Cayuse Indians on a bend of the Walla Walla River in 1837. Two years later the Reverend Cushing Eells and his wife, Myra, visited the struggling little farm. Built of adobe, the mission home had doors and window-frames made of hand-hewn boards. Myra Eells noted the farm had wheat, corn and potato fields, and gardens with vegetables and melons.

By 1844 the productive mission farm and sawmill attracted many emigrants, with about fifteen hundred people stopping that year. The Whitmans took in the seven Sager children, left orphaned as their family followed the trail and immortalized in the book *On to Oregon.* Mary Ann Bridger, daughter of Jim Bridger, and Helen Mar Meek, daughter of mountain man Joe Meek, also lived with the Whitmans.

In November 1847, a band of emigrants visited the mission. They had the measles, which they passed on to some of the mission children, and to the Cayuse Indians, who had no resistance to most of the diseases of the white people. Although Dr. Whitman treated all of the children, and some of them recovered, more than half of the Indian children died. The tribal members blamed Whitman, saying he was administering poison.

On November 29, 1847, Dr. Whitman conducted services for three children of a Cayuse chief who had died of the

*With his flag flying, Earl Leggett and the Aurora wagon cross eastern Oregon, re-enacting the journey of the Keil family, carrying the casket of Willie Keil.* (Bill White Photo)

measles. Just after lunch the Indians retaliated against the mission and its leaders. They killed Dr. Whitman while he was getting medicine for one of the Indians. Many other children and adults, including three of the Sager children and Mrs. Whitman, also died in the attack. Helen Meek, who was ill at the time, died when there was no one left to care for her, and Mary Ann Bridger died the next year.

The Indians captured three people and held them for ransom. They burned the mission buildings and cut down the orchard. The captives eventually were ransomed. Joe Meek seized the opportunity and went to Washington where he convinced Congress that the white people in Oregon needed protection. Congress granted territorial status without delay. No one re-established the mission.

So only in the earliest years of trail travel did emigrants visit the Walla Walla Mission. Instead travelers headed to the Umatilla Indian Agency and after 1855 to the Fort Henrietta military stockade. The travelers crossed Echo Meadows and prepared themselves for the dry and dusty road to the John Day and Deschutes Rivers.

BEN KERN:

BK Sept. 24. Left Pendleton for Echo. We saw Mount Hood today. Its top is socked in.

BK Sept. 25. Left Echo. We crossed some dry, dusty country today. A lot of onions in this country and Bobby stopped and picked some from a farmer's field for us to eat. We got new cooks at Eagle, Idaho. One of them, John, is a retired veterinarian. We are camped on a place owned by some wheat farmers. There are some peach trees here and the peaches had fallen off. When the cooks got in this afternoon they gathered up these peaches and made a peach cobbler. Had a real nice supper. Then John said, "Guess we'd better have a little dessert." He had gone into town and bought ice cream and here he came with this great big old peach cobbler and ice cream. This place is way up on a big high hill and there is a full moon. It is just like daylight, and you can look out and see Mount Hood. We saw Mount Hood during the day, but actually it is more clear in the moonlight.

BK Sept. 26. Came to Cecil. Another day over dry country. Bad camp place. These ranchers brought their sheep in off the Blues and they have about 3,000 lambs in a lot right beside us and it is dusty. The dust is everyplace. They don't make much noise although we can hear them blatting at times. They aren't bawling constantly or anything. They are just milling. Cecil is just a wide spot in the road, a little store. They really gave us a big feed tonight.

EARL LEGGETT:

EL We come through when all the fruit was ripe, Bobby would be picking apples off the trees. He'd be picking onions out of someone's onion patch. He'd give us an apple, or a raw onion to eat. I said he would be in jail.

All along the route I haven't seen much wildlife. I am surprised at that, too, because you would have thought that at the speed we are traveling we would have seen lots and lots more antelope and we really seen very few compared to the miles that we traveled and the locale that we traveled in.

We seen some jack rabbits but not a lot. I don't know that maybe I've seen over three or four coyotes in our whole trip. I didn't hear the coyotes, but maybe it was because I was snoring or something. Generally I would listen at night, I didn't hear them. I don't think I ever heard them calling for one another all the time I came across.

THE ECHO MEADOW crossing usually took place in late August and early September, when temperatures soared to nearly 100 degrees daily. The trail through this country is little changed, with the ruts still deep concaves in the sandy soil, covered with sage and grasses of the desert topography.

From Echo Meadow, the trail crosses the Boardman segment, now a part of the Boardman Bombing Range—an aerial gunning range—operated by the U.S. Department of the Navy. Here the trail is as it was in history. It crosses no paved roads, nor any other sign of civilization. It does cross several intermittent streams and is a well-defined pattern in the soil. The land is pretty stark, and in emigrant days this was one of the driest stretches the travelers crossed. The Boeing Company leased a portion of this route in the early 1980s for use as a rocket testing area.

Once across the desert-like range along the Boardman segment of the trail, the Oregon pathway enters rolling country, intersected by small canyons, like Fourmile Canyon. Although much of this area is now turned to agricultural production, some original trail segments remain.

BEN KERN:

BK Sept. 27. We left Cecil and came to McDonald Ford, the crossing of the John Day River. Forded the river. No trouble. The water barely reached the horses' knees.

BY THE TIME TRAVELERS reached the John Day River, they were ready to rejoice at the sight of fresh water. John C. Frémont in 1843 wrote, "At noon we crossed John Day's river, a clear and beautiful stream, with a swift current and a bed of rolled stones. It is sunk in a deep valley, which is characteristic of all streams in this region."

The McDonald Ford, about nineteen miles west of Fourmile Canyon, marked the crossing of the first of several major rivers flowing north toward the Columbia. The travelers must have realized their goal was in sight as they watched the water flowing toward the north and west, rather than the south and east.

Trail ruts mark the hills above the John Day River and the McDonald Ford is relatively unspoiled by the passage of time. After crossing the McDonald Ford, the trail winds through the hills toward the Columbia River, topping out on a ridge with a broad vista of Oregon spread before the wagons. From the high road, Mount Hood to the west and the Columbia River to the north and flowing west, become markers by which to reckon.

Not much remains of the original trail here, and the scenery is somewhat spoiled by powerlines, highways, and railroad right-of-ways. Most of the ruts are under the concrete and tracks for cars and trains.

**Ben Kern:**

BK Sept. 28. We came to Wasco. We are camped by the church. Went to the school for showers. They put on a feed, both supper and breakfast.

BK Sept. 29. We left for Deschutes. Really a nice campground at Deschutes State Park right on the river.

BK Sept. 30. Left Deschutes and headed for The Dalles. Pretty route. Climbed up on the bench and we were on the bench above the Columbia River. You could look up and down the Columbia four or five miles both ways. Lots of boats on the river. The wind blowed real hard. Real pretty view. We were supposed to stop by this school and be in at 10:30 and we pulled in to the school yard and they had cookies and punch. All the kids come out and visited with us, petted the horses. One of the teachers made an announcement. We traveled five months and were fifteen minutes late. Left The Dalles and came to Creits Point. Had a celebration, old time music, big feed.

The Dalles started as a mission operated by Methodist Missionary Daniel Lee in 1838. His mission, which by 1843 had five buildings, served as a stopping place and way station for emigrants until its abandonment in 1847.

The assistance they found no doubt saved the lives of many of the unfortunate group of emigrants who left the Oregon Trail at Vale, Oregon, in 1845, to follow Meek's Cutoff. The venture, like that of the Donner party, turned into near tragedy as the people became isolated and stranded. Their arrival at Lee's Mission at The Dalles meant survival. As Samuel Parker wrote on October 7, 1845, of the trip over Meek's Cutoff, "I will just say pen & tongue will both fall short when they go to tell the suffering the company went through. There my wife and child died."

John C. Frémont explained the origin of the name for the mission, fort, and eventually the community, this way: "*The Dalles of the Columbia.* The whole volume of the river at this place passes between the walls of a chasm, which has the appearance of having been rent through the basaltic strata which form the valley rock of the region. At the narrowest... the average height of the walls above the water is 25 feet; forming a trough between the rocks—hence the name, probably applied by a Canadian voyager."

Following the 1847 fight at the Whitman Mission, volunteer troops built a stockade at The Dalles. In May 1850 the military converted the site into a regular U.S. Army post and called it Camp Drum. It became Fort Dalles in 1853, occupied by two companies of the Regiment of Mountain Riflemen, whose purpose was to protect emigrants on the Oregon Trail.

Fort Dalles eventually had eight army companies and a dozen buildings in which to house the operations. For a time it was the only military post on the trail between Fort Laramie and Fort Vancouver. It became a quartermaster's depot in 1861. The army abandoned the post in 1867.

The site eventually evolved into the present city of The Dalles, which is dwarfed today by a dam, a set of locks, and a power plant across the Columbia River. Huge concrete bastions hold heavy wires and cables where man has harnessed the mighty Columbia for power.

At The Dalles, the historic travelers had a choice to make—one route included a turbulent ride down the Columbia while the other route presented an equally treacherous crossing over the Cascades on the Barlow Toll Road. Many of the travelers who chose the river route engaged passage down the Columbia in canoes built and handled by local Indians. They left behind their wagons which had served as homes for months.

Often the trip turned to one of great hazard as high winds rocked the waters, forming great waves from the ocean. The scenery was, and remains, spectacular. The wide, flowing river and the high cliffs and waterfalls of the river canyon area provide many magnificent views.

At the Cascades of the Columbia, some travelers tempted fate and rode the rapids on loaded boats, but many unloaded and resorted to a back-breaking portage some three to five miles long. They carried their goods along the raging waters of the Columbia.

The river flows placidly these days because a series of dams and locks on the channel have tamed it from a free-flowing waterway to a kind of long, narrow reservoir. Bridges periodically provide crossing points between Oregon and Washington. Nearer to the mouth of the Columbia, the water is more turbulent, giving a sense of what it might have been like in the days of the emigrants.

Those who avoided the Columbia by traveling the Barlow Toll Road had a hazardous trek as well. Samuel K. Barlow and Joel Palmer blazed the road across the shoulder of Mount Hood in 1845 as an alternative to the Columbia River route. The Barlow Toll Road operated from 1846 until 1919.

Abigail Scott Duniway in 1852 had a recipe for Barlow Road soup. In it she called for people to "boil an antiquated ham bone. Add to the liquid the few scrapings from the dough pan in which you mixed the biscuit from your last measure of flour, which by now will be musty and sour. If you have no bone, thicken some water from flour shaken from a remaining flour sack."

The travelers on the 1993 wagon train veered from the Columbia at The Dalles, and took the mountain route over the Barlow Road to the Willamette valley.

BEN KERN:

BK Oct. 1. Left Creits Point headed for Dufur. We were on pavement all day and had a police escort to direct traffic. We had three long hills to climb today. We stopped for lunch at a wide turnout on the highway.

BK Oct. 2. To Tyge Valley. We stayed at the rodeo grounds. I had picked up for rodeos at Tyge Valley in earlier years. I started rodeoing in Wyoming before I went in the service, then I spent some time in Wyoming before migrating to Oregon where I rodeoed in 1948–1949. I rode bareback broncs and when I decided not to compete any longer, I started working for various contractors as a pick-up man, snagging cowboys from the backs of bucking horses at rodeos throughout Oregon. I picked up for Harley Tucker, a great stock contractor from Joseph, Oregon, and I picked up for the Christensen Brothers of Eugene. One year I even picked up for the Pendleton Roundup.

BK Oct. 3. Left Tyge and headed for Rock Creek Reservoir. Going up the grade we went on the oiled highway, but you can look up the hill and see the original ruts all the way up the hill, they're very distinct here. Its rocky and now there are scattered trees in the area. When we topped out, we could see the ruts meandering alongside the road. This morning a bunch of Indians in an old pickup run right in front of me and about cut me off as I started. They said we could not go on the Barlow Trail. They said it was their sacred ground. We will by-pass that part of the trail. A lot of horseback riders joined us here.

AS THE TRAIN CROSSED Idaho and Oregon, Ben had lots of relatives to "get shook out of the weeds," according to Earl. "Even in this part of the country we still had people coming out of the brush and out of the clumps of grass" to visit Ben.

There is a thirty-two mile segment of Oregon Trail from Barlow Gate on the eastern edge of the Mount Hood National Forest to the western Barlow Tollgate. For most of the distance, the Barlow Road exists as either a dirt road or a forest trail. It is the best-preserved segment of the Oregon Trail in Oregon and winds through huge, old growth forest.

Much of the route is crossed today only with horses and wagons, or by hikers wanting and willing to trek over such a route. The Forest Service does not allow vehicles over this segment of trail. The huge old trees, some of them scarred from earlier travelers' wagon wheels, block the sun from the trail.

BEN KERN:

BK Oct. 4. Left Rock Creek Reservoir headed for White River Camp. About 4–5 miles up we hit the Barlow Trail from The Dalles, really got into the timber and the real thick part of it and out away from the highway about 4–5 miles from Rock Creek. We were out-of-sight and out-of-mind all the way through there. All kinds of trees, Douglas fir, Red fir, and Pine. The nights get cold up here and already the leaves of some trees are turning red and gold.

BK Oct. 5. Came from White River Camp to Summit Meadow Camp. Before we reached Summit Meadow, we saw a big lake below camp. We crossed the dam by the lake and could see Mount Hood reflected in the water.

THE BARLOW ROAD reaches the summit of the Cascade Mountains at Barlow Pass, and to the west the trail cuts through the forest and mountain meadows. Summit Meadow provided feed for stock, particularly needed during the period of emigration, because by the time the animals reached this final mountain pass, they were in poor shape.

*The 1993 travelers cross Oregon, with Mount Hood in the background.* (Bill White Photo)

By contrast, the animals on the train Ben traveled with were in better shape in western Oregon than they had been in central Wyoming. They'd eaten increased feed and had additional vitamins and minerals. Some of the animals even had a period of rest, when they were loaded in horse trailers and hauled back to Wyoming pastures to recover from sores rubbed by the collars and harnesses. After building strength they returned to the trail.

One of the major challenges on the Barlow Road was the crossing of Laurel Hill, considered by many to be the most difficult hill on the entire Oregon Trail. By the time they reached that point on the two thousand mile journey, exhaustion affected both people and animals.

An 1853 emigrant wrote that the road on Laurel Hill "is something terrible." By that time the trail cut down into the soil from five to seven feet. Steep banks flanked both sides, and the trace became so narrow, people found it difficult to walk alongside their oxen. In cases they had to lean against the animals in order to squeeze through the trees.

*"Barlow Cutoff" by William Henry Jackson. Named for Samuel K. Barlow, an early pioneer from Kentucky, this portion of the road was actually a tollway near Mt. Hood in Oregon.* (Courtesy Scotts Bluff National Monument)

The tired travelers rough-locked their wagon wheels by tying trees to them to prevent their turning. Emigrants also tied long ropes to the rear axles which anchored the wagons to trees to slow the descent.

Ben's horses were fat and sassy as they headed down from Summit Meadow into the Willamette valley. Their brown-black coats shiny and growing thicker as temperatures continued to drop.

EARL LEGGETT:

EL — That first full day's pull on the Barlow was probably one of the hardest pulls we had on the whole trip. We didn't have a lot of hot weather, but as we crossed the Barlow Road, it was pretty hot and we had a lot of upgrade to pull that day. It was probably one of our hardest pull days of the whole thing. It could have been because we were so close to the end of the journey that we were so anxious that it felt that way.

The terrain was pretty much enclosed with big firs and pines and brush and underbrush and the road was just cut out for the trail and it's been there ever since.

BEN KERN:

BK Oct. 6. Left Summit Meadow. It's snowing. Went to Brightwood, camped right in Main Street. A couple that owned the bar were deer hunting at Rock Creek Reservoir when we passed by and they told Earl and I they had a place for us to stay here in Brightwood. The back door of the bar, they had roped it all off and that's where we kept the horses. So we just stepped out of the bar to take care of them.

The people had a fancy motor home backed out there by the horses and said to Earl and I, "This is where you guys are going to stay." It was all stocked with beer. It rained. Really bad rain. Laid over a day. We took one wagon and a team and went to the ski lodge at Government Camp and had lunch up there on Mount Hood. It snowed on us.

BK Oct. 9. Left Brightwood and went to Sandy. Stayed on a rancher's place. Big feed. Big supper.

BK Oct. 10. Left Sandy for Estacada then Oregon City.

AS THEY CROSSED THE Cascades, the last mountain range on their long journey, the emigrants saw before them, finally, the Willamette valley.

"It resembled an enchanted valley as we wound around the hill before descending into it," Lucia Lorain Williams wrote in 1851.

BEN KERN:

BK Oct. 11. Camped at Oregon City. This was a big celebration. We stayed in the park. They had a dedication and big feed. All the food related to the type the emigrants might have had on the wagon trains like homemade butter. One gal made home brew and had it in quart fruit jars. It was good. Had ham hock and beans, homemade bread, fried bread, fried potatoes, fried squash, hominy and homemade ice cream.

THE HISTORIC TRAIL ended at Oregon City. After at least five months spent crossing the plains of Kansas and Nebraska where thousands died of Asiatic Cholera, the sage and mountains and alkali desert of Wyoming and Idaho, and finally the treacherous mountains and rivers of Oregon they reached the trail's end.

There the emigrants traded their wagons for crude homes and started to carve a new life in their new land. Dr. John McLoughlin, chief factor of the Hudson's Bay Company, established Oregon City in 1842. He was administrator of Fort Vancouver and benefactor to many of the impoverished emigrants who arrived on his doorstep in Oregon City starting in 1843.

Sarah Cummins wrote upon reaching Oregon City in 1845: "The environs of our new home, surrounded by giant fur trees, the healthful sea breezes, the strange sights and sounds were sources of continual thought. The long distance that separated us from our old home in the Mississippi Valley, precluded any form of home sickness and our united efforts were wholly set upon the building of a home."

The women who made the trip had little sense of relief when they arrived in Oregon. They camped along the river bottom, but had no homes. They still lived in their wagons and tents and complained of constant drizzle and fog. To them the weather was "dark and gloomy."

Marilla R. Washburn Bailey wrote in 1852, when she was thirteen: "My most vivid recollection of that first winter in Oregon is of the weeping skies and of Mother and me also weeping."

*The huge, old fir and pine trees along the Barlow Road dwarf the teams and wagons on the sesquicentennial train.* (Bill White Photo)

But like they'd done on the entire trip, most of the women held their chins up and put on their best faces. They took the gay-colored quilts that had protected cherished dishes and other treasures in the wagons and placed the quilts on new beds. Bibles and photographs took their places on new, crude cabin shelves.

BEN KERN:

BK Oct. 12. Left Oregon City and traveled to Canby, where we stayed the night.

BK Oct. 13. Earl led the wagons into Aurora today. This is his home. There are a lot of people to meet us. More people here than anywhere else on the trail. We stayed in the park, kept our horses right here in the park, too.

BK Oct. 14. Had a celebration in Aurora. Earl gave me a plaque. It says, "Ben Kern, your loyalty and friendship will long be remembered."

Reaching Aurora marked a milestone for Earl. He'd brought Willie Keil home symbolically, traveling the ruts of the Oregon Trail as the original Aurora Colony pioneers had done. Earl had made the trip on the seat of an historic Aurora Colony wagon pulled by Sue and Ann, a team of mules.

As the train neared Aurora, Earl said:

EL When we pulled (near) Aurora several people asked me if Willie's wagon was going to be leading the wagon train when it gets into Aurora tomorrow, and I said I don't know.... The morning we pulled out it was raining very hard, my wife was riding with me and...Shawn rode by and he said, "When we get to Barlow and we pull out of there, put Sue and Ann up front."

We pulled out of the Barlow cemetery and it was funny because all the wagons were sitting there and we'd always been the fifth wagon back following down the trail. I put Sue and Ann around the wagons and up front and they're looking around at me like there's something wrong here. [As if to ask] what are we doing up here, you know. They're just easing along, any other time they'd be clipping right along, but they're just easing along because they're not sure if they should be up there in front.

We pulled over the hill and you could see the people that were standing there in the rain with their umbrellas. It was all worth the trip. This is what it'd been all about.

Every morning when I got up I told myself we had a job to do and a goal, this was the day that we had been getting up every morning for. It was raining. It was raining the day we pulled out of Independence so why should it be any different when we pulled into Aurora. It gives me a sense of accomplishment not only for myself, but for everyone who traveled the trail.

I feel pride, too, for the community of Aurora to accomplish what it did. Having fund raisers to get across country on this trip. Donations and fund raisers. That's the way we bought the harness. That's the way we bought the mules. That's how this country was built originally and so in 1993 it gives you a sense of pride that that's the way it can still be done, the way it was done in 1843.

ALTHOUGH ORIGINALLY Earl planned to remain in Aurora while the other wagons went on to Independence, Oregon, when they reached his hometown, Earl decided to continue the trip. "I become part of that family, had gained their respect, and they wanted me to go on to Independence," he said.

BEN KERN:

BK Oct. 15. Left Aurora and came to Champoeg. A neat place. A fruit farm. They have acres and acres and acres of pumpkins. We camped way back in the back, back out through the pumpkin patch. People come out and use wheelbarrows and load them up with pumpkins. They have a bee tree and have a glass tube from a hole in the tree. Here's the bees working coming up and down that tube. All day long kids watched them bees come up and down that tube. Lots of vegetables. Laid over at Champoeg.

BK Oct. 18. Left Champoeg and came to St. Paul. Camped at the rodeo grounds. I'd picked up for rodeos here, too, and had supper with the rodeo association members and swapped old tales.

BK Oct. 19. Left St. Paul for Salem. We pulled up in front of the Capitol building had lunch and a dedication on the

Capitol steps. They had great big plastic tubs on a framework with rollers and they rolled them out for water for the horses. It was really neat. We headed on out of town to camp at Rickreall at the fairgrounds.

CANDY MOULTON:

CM Oregon's capitol city of Salem gave the wagon train a huge welcome when thousands of people—including more than one thousand children for whom school was dismissed—lined the streets on October 19. From Salem the train went to Rickreall and then to Dallas. It included the five wagons, which started the trip in Independence, Missouri, and three additional wagons, which joined in Oregon.

Twenty-one hours in a car had left me tired and anxious as I rolled into Salem to join the wagons for the final few days. As Ben participated in the final big celebration in Salem, I studied a map to figure out how to find the wagons. The city is so much bigger than I expected. Whenever I joined the wagon train during the past five months, I'd never had any difficulty locating them. I'd watch the trail.

Horse and mule manure always served as the first sign, then perhaps I'd see the rocking, dipping white canvas of the wagon tops, or sometimes the conical Indian-style tipis always set up in camp. In Salem I found that impossible, but I marked a route on a city map and headed west.

Just out of Salem, traffic snarled and finally, near a golf course, I caught sight of the wagons. A lump grew in my throat as I passed them by, parked my car, grabbed my cameras, and headed toward the highway. Although I needed to take photos, I was overwhelmed by seeing the friends I'd made on this trip.

Ben lead the way with Mark and Mike. Then came the girls, Marie, Leeann, Erin, Kris, with their three wagons. They each

*Ben Kern in Independence, Oregon, holding some of the mail he carried in his wagon for six months in making a delivery from Independence, Missouri.* (Candy Moulton Photo)

asked if I wanted to ride, and I reluctantly declined, since I'd parked my car only a few hundred yards away. Shawn rode by on a zebra dun mule, and I turned to follow the wagons back to my vehicle, when I heard a whistle and a comment behind my back: "I recognize that hat." I recognized that voice and turned to greet Dave Bowhay who, like me, had traveled hundreds of miles to be with this train as it reached its final destination.

We camped at the fairgrounds in Rickreall, and it didn't seem like the same wagon train I'd been with earlier. The presence of hot showers and electrical outlets, combined with the steady traffic by the fairgrounds, was so different from early days I spent with the wagon train when we camped in sagebrush and slopped through mud as rain dripped from our hats.

**Ben Kern:**

BK Oct. 20. A short trip from Rickreall to Dallas. We're camped in a field. Lots of yellowjackets.

BK Oct. 21. Riding to Independence there aren't as many people as we saw in Aurora. We went through Monmoth, where Shawn got into an argument with the mayor and another wagon train, the Applegate Wagon Train. The argument involved whether both wagon trains would travel together to Independence and who would lead the way. Finally we decided the eight wagons in our train would join the Applegate wagons for the last few miles into Independence, and I led the way as I had since Missouri.

We did it. I am disappointed in a way. I thought there'd be more people here. Independence didn't turn out like I thought it would. Actually our ending is just a big argument. I'm happy that we came all the way. As far as the celebration and reception, it isn't that great.

**Candy Moulton:**

CM Only dim shadows covered the land as we ate breakfast October 21 in an open field on the west side of Dallas. To the north were houses and to the south a sawmill, where workers turned the mighty pines of the northwest into lumber for homes and other materials. The field was grassy, but deceptive as it was filled with underground pockets of yellowjackets that flew up furious when trod upon.

As drivers hitched the horses and mules for the final drive into Independence, the sun warmed our backs. The camp had a somber mood; people realized they'd reached the end of their

*The 1993 train decided to go all the way to the coast and test the water at Canon Beach, Oregon.* (Bill White Photo)

trip. When the wagons circled out of camp, fog rolled in from the coast and the sawmill became a ghost in its mists. The wagon wheels rolled through Dallas, headed toward Independence, and the temperature dropped.

I rode with Kris. It is where I chose to be. I rode with her my first day on the train, and I wanted to be with her as we reached the end of the route. She put on a Hudson Bay style capote and tied the hood over her long auburn hair. I zipped my down jacket and searched for a pair of gloves, as the temperature dropped and the fog turned to misty rain.

It was right that the weather turned to this dampness. When Kris and I rode together in Nebraska, we huddled under a tattered quilt and watched the rain drip from our hats.

Shortly before noon, we rolled into Independence. I moved to the back of the wagon, and Dan Naffsinger sat beside Kris. It was his rightful place; he and his wife Juleen had joined the wagons in Missouri and had covered the entire distance of this trek with the wagon train. After a short stop in the city park, the wagons drove through town and delivered mail carried in Ben's wagon since the trip's beginning May 2.

This wagon train traveled twenty-three hundred miles through six states in rain, hail, snow, tornadoes, and dust. Along the route, it lost three animals and a lot of help quit. Those on the train also became ill with colds and flu and more than once someone had to get help from a doctor or a hospital. Support crew workers—those people who set up camp, cooked, and helped with the chores—came and went, and none of those who started the trip finished. Nearly a dozen cooks tended the pots.

BEN KERN:

BK October 22. We laid over here in Independence a couple of days. Earl left to go home. When Earl got ready to leave that was really tough, I went over and they were loading the mules, Sue and Ann. I told Earl this is no time for being sad or anything else. We're gonna see each other. We just shook hands real quick and he jumped in his rig and left.

Earl had a difficult time making the split with Ben, too. Another wrenching goodbye came even later when he parted from the mules, Sue and Ann. He said:

EL The day that we had to sell them, because they belonged to the Chamber of Commerce in Aurora, it was a sad day in my life because they were part of my family. We spent from the 8th of March to the 21st of October together... a lot of miles and a lot of trust was built.

*The end of the trail brought conflicting emotions.* (Bill White Photo)

I know more so probably now than what I did out on the trail, the appreciation people had . . . for us keeping history alive.

The last thought I've tried to leave with people is for them, if they have an opportunity to do so, to pass some history along, don't pass that opportunity up.

For me, the partings weren't any easier. This is my last journal entry of that trip:

CM October 22, 1993. My birthday and I celebrate by myself on the banks of the Willamette River in Independence, Oregon. I've just completed a wonderful journey. Rich in experience, equally rich in friendships forged. On this date in 1812 Robert Stuart and six companions stumbled upon the broad swale of South Pass that became the key to western migration.

We have seen the elephant.

APPENDIX:

# Goodale Cutoff

*"A day's ride is like a little piece of heaven."*
—Ben Kern, 1994

The 1993 sesquicentennial wagon train did not travel the Goodale Cutoff in Idaho, but chose to remain on the primary route. The following summer, in 1994, Ben Kern was invited to join a wagon train which planned to travel the Goodale Cutoff segment of the trail. Ben saw this as an opportunity to make his Oregon Trail experience even more complete. This trek, not bound by the tight time constraints of the pioneers or the sesquicentennial train, took on a more leisurely, relaxed atmosphere. So June 1, 1994, found Ben joining new companions to start a fresh adventure.

From Fort Hall, Goodale's Cutoff headed north and then west past what is now Craters of the Moon National Monument. The cutoff went through Boise and on to the Payette and Weiser River country before heading north into Oregon. The Goodale Cutoff became particularly popular after miners discovered gold in northern Idaho in 1862.

Tim Goodale pioneered the route when he steered wagons north of Massacre Rocks on the main branch of the Oregon Trail. Nathan Hall, founder of Fort Hall, also used the route as a supply line to the mouth of the Columbia River. Nathaniel Wyeth made the first documented crossing on the route in 1834. It is now embraced by the Idaho National Engineering Laboratory.

BK June 1, 1994. I left Casper at 4 in the afternoon headed for Arco, Idaho, to meet with Les Broadie to put the Goodale wagon train together. I got into Arco, about 2 in the morning at the Blizzard Mountain Ranch where Les lived. I slept in my pickup until about 6 o'clock, when Les come out and woke me up. This is the first time I met Les and his wife Ruth. We had a real good breakfast and started making plans for the wagon train.

Les appointed me trail boss so we started putting things together. We had to go over quite a bit of the trail, which we started doing. We started putting the wagons together and getting supplies.

BK June 2–9. George Roberts from Riggins, Idaho, came in. He had a sheep wagon and he had four head of horses and they had been saddle horses, but had never been worked very much for pulling a wagon. So I worked with George driving his horses. We had some pretty exciting days a time or two before we got them where they would work, but they finally turned out where they would work pretty good.

Les had two real nice teams of mules, one blond team and one blue roan team, and they had been out on the mountain all winter when I gathered them in. Les had two young colts that had been started, so I started riding them, too. We'd work 'em a couple hours a day. Every day.

Les had two real nice wagons. One was a brand new wagon, a chuck wagon, it'd never been pulled. The other was only about two years old, had good covers for them. We had flys to pull out over the chuck box to make our kitchen. And we had canvas to close the wagon in on each end. They were really nice wagons.

Dave "Skinner" Collins from Heber, Idaho, came to the ranch on the 7th of June. He is a horse shoer and he will go on the wagon train with us. He shod all the mules, he shod the horses, and he is a real good guy to work with.

BK June 10–12. We had everything pretty well put together and ready to go on the 10th of June. We loaded our wagons on a trailer. We are going to haul them to our starting point. We loaded our horses and we headed for Springfield, on the Snake River by Fort Hall. That is where we will begin our trip.

We got into Springfield late in the afternoon, started setting up camp. We have a set of corrals for our livestock, have plenty of water, and we have hay here. Set up camp, I set up my dutch ovens to do the cooking. I will do a lot of the cooking.

When we got into Springfield a lot of the other people had arrived, there are about fifteen wagons all together and everybody has pretty well set up their camps and put everything together.

The 14th is the day we are going to leave, so we have a few days to lay around. We made acquaintance with everybody and made plans about how we are going to go over the trail. There are a lot of nice people going with us. We are having a lot of fun. Take turns cooking supper. At night we go to different wagons. Have a lot of good cooks on the wagon train.

BK June 13. I put on a big stew in one of my dutch ovens, cooked it all day and tonight everybody came over and had supper with us and we made plans for departing tomorrow morning. I will tell you how to make a stew. I put all my vegetables in like potatoes, onions, carrots, and celery, and canned tomatoes and I like to put a little can of V-8 juice in it and lots of garlic. I use lots of garlic. Sometimes I put turnips in.

I like to take the stew meat and sprinkle chili powder over the meat and lots of salt and pepper then I brown it real good. When it's browned real good, after the stew vegetables have cooked a little while, I put the meat in. I let it cook most of the day and not long before I serve it, I add a little brown sugar and that makes it really, really good.

BK June 14. We left. We pulled out of camp this morning about 7 o'clock. It was kind of exciting. A lot of the horses hadn't been worked all that much and we had a couple of runaways. No real big mishaps. One of the gals that was an outrider got bucked off. It was kind of exciting. We got off to a really good start.

It was hot and dry today and we started across the desert headed for Wheatgrass Wells. We killed about fifteen rattlesnakes. The rattlesnakes were really thick on the desert. Everybody had to be really careful. Nobody wants to sleep on the ground. They are kind of hesitant about that. We got into our first camp about 4 this afternoon it was a pretty long day for the first day. Our camp is around some water tanks. It is pretty dry and a dusty old camp.

BK June 15. We pulled out of camp. We have 13 miles to do today. We are headed toward Frenchman Cabin which is at the base of the big Southern Butte and that is a big landmark out on the desert. That's out on the Snake River Plains. It goes from the desert floor to about 5,000 feet, so it is quite a landmark and there is a small herd of elk that stay out here.

We got into Frenchman Cabin about 2 this afternoon. Had a set of corrals to put our livestock in. This used to be a stage station, so had good corrals, a lot of water, it was a pretty good place to camp. The log barn here at Frenchman Cabin was built of logs from Big Butte.

Years ago when the stage station was here they piped the water in a wooden pipeline from the spring, and we went with a BLM employee up to see some of the old wooden line. They had a big cistern down at the station where they stored the water. We had a good supper tonight. Everybody pitched in and cooked up different dishes. Mrs. Fielding from Washington baked bread so we really had a good feast tonight.

BK June 16. We pulled out of camp headed for Arco, which was 20 miles. Today we had to go across [Idaho National Engineering Laboratory] Atomic Energy property and so we had to have escorts from Atomic Energy staff to go across their property. This was really an interesting trip today. We were on the old original trail and the people from the Atomic Energy put on a program for us. We got into Arco about 4 in the afternoon. We stayed at the Fairgrounds. The citizens of Arco put on a real good feed for us tonight and we had a band.

BK June 17. The city of Arco cooked breakfast for us and we left Arco headed for Martin's Cove, on Les Broadie's Blizzard Mountain Ranch. We got in here about 3 in the afternoon and there was a lot of people waiting here for us. The park service put on a program for us. They catered a meal for us and tonight they fed about 600 people.

Martin's Cove was a townsite at one time. They had a post office here and a stage station. Mrs. Martin run the post office for about 30 years and she was 82 years old when they shut the post office down. There was an old pear tree here, still growing. Mrs. Martin had a garden out back of the post office, and we can see the asparagus coming up and growing.

BK June 18. We're staying here at Martin's Cove today. There's a gravesite of a little girl that got bit by a rattlesnake out by the big buttes, out by Frenchman Cabin, and she lived until they got here at Martin's Cove. We fenced the gravesite. We put up a real nice fence and a plaque on the gravesite. We put up a historical marker and a plaque that tells about the Martin townsite history.

We went to town and bought supplies and got ready to go on to the next campsite.

BK June 19. We left Martin's Cove this morning and we're headed for our next camp, Big Cottonwood. Today we went across Craters of the Moon National Monument and this was a real interesting part of the trail. Lots of lava rock and pretty rough trail. We got into Big Cottonwood about 3 in the afternoon. This was an original camp, lots of cottonwood groves, lots of water. This is a good camp site. Here at Big Cottonwood is right on the trail where the Indians came through. They would come off of the Snake River Plains and come through the Craters of the Moon and head back for the mountains.

BK June 20. We broke camp here at Big Cottonwood this morning and headed for Lava Lake. We got about 13 miles to go today. A rancher near here had just trailed in a bunch of cattle down the old original wagon ruts so they really had it stirred up. It was really hot and dry and dusty and the wind blowed today. It was really kind of a bad day today.

We got into Lava Lake at 3 in the afternoon and not too far from the lake here is a big hot springs and there's a big pool down by the hot springs and everybody enjoyed a good bath tonight. Les Broadie, the wagon boss, said he was going to take all the girls up to the swimming pool and take a bath.

BK June 21. We left Lava Lake this morning. We had about 12 miles to go today. Got in early today, had a real nice place to camp. The rancher where we camped barbecued a pig and some chickens. He butchered the hog on the ranch and then took the hide and fat and made cracklins so we had beer and cracklins. This is a combination hereford ranch and dairy ranch and at supper they set big pitchers of fresh milk on the table. They had a band and we really had a good time.

BK June 22. Left for Point of Rock. This was a real steep trail today, rough and rocky and we went over what they call Barton Pass. Right there at the summit there's two gravesites. There's an Indian buried there and a cavalry soldier buried there and we put fences around the sites. We had about 9 miles today. Got into Point of Rock early.

BK June 23-24. We left Point of Rock this morning and we headed for another ranch just out of Bellevue, Idaho. We got in early this afternoon and we have a set of corrals and lots of water for our livestock. This is a real good campsite. We're going to lay over here three days and rest up.

BK Sunday June 25. This was a real good day. The southern Idaho Draft Horse Association came out and spent the day with us and they cooked our supper. They barbecued chicken, and had salads and watermelon.

BK June 26. We broke camp this morning and headed for Shirley Springs. We have 15 miles to go today. Rough trail today, pretty steep and rocky. We had a runaway today. Spooked one of the outfits and didn't hurt anything too bad, but it made for a little excitement. We got into Shirley Springs midafternoon.

Awful hot and dry here. We had a few shade trees and a little bit of water, not a whole lot of water here. We had a lot of company along towards evening. Some of the ranchers turned about 800 head of cows in the pasture that we were camped in and so we had a lot of company all night. The cows thought our camp was kind of interesting.

Skinner and I are kind of the camp tenders. We get up every morning at 4:30. He waters the mules and tends them. I start the fire and usually cook breakfast. Then Skinner harnesses the teams while Ruth, the girls from England, and a gal from Portland, Oregon, do the dishes. We clean up the camp and that way we are ready to roll out of camp about 7 in the morning. We have pretty short runs, but we like to get up early and go so we can get into camp before it gets real hot. Last year my trip was pretty cold and rainy. This year it has been hot and dry.

BK June 27. I fried bacon and eggs and had sourdough pancakes so we had a good breakfast this morning. We're headed for Butte Springs today, that's our next campsite. This is an old townsite. The old town of Creighton. Some of the old buildings are still here. The people that own the ranch here have an old farm machinery collection and he's really got quite an accumulation. Some of the old stuff goes back quite a lot of years.

BK June 28. We broke camp this morning and headed for Fairfield. Only got 8 miles to go today. Got in about 1 o'clock. Camped at the Park and kept our livestock at the Forest Service compound. We kind of laid around this afternoon and took it easy. Tonight the Southern Idaho Fiddlers Association came out and played music for us. Had a lot of good fiddling music and had a good time.

Fairfield, Idaho, is in the center of Camas Prairie, which is really a big area where the Indians used to come and pick the Camas bulbs that they used for herbs. A lady told me in later years there was a poisonous camas plant, so now most of them are poisons, so you've got to be careful when you're picking them. Camas Prairie is really a big hay producing area. There's a lot of cranes in the area. Every morning we'd get up and there'd be big flocks of cranes. This is a big nesting area for them.

BK June 29. We broke camp this morning. Left Fairfield and we're headed for Cow Creek Reservoir. Got about 18 miles to go today. This is an area out around Cow Creek that's really hit bad by the drought. This is a big reservoir, but it's almost dry this year. We got into Cow Creek Reservoir about 5 today and we have a good campsite. Have some corrals to use, they are old corrals. We have a pretty good place to put our livestock.

I bought a bunch of steaks at Fairfield. I marinated them in some Tequila. Tonight we piled up some rocks and made a fire and put a screen across the rocks then fried up those steaks. They were awfully tender and good. We had a family from India join us. They were on a tour of the United States. They had beer and all kinds of food, fresh tomatoes, cantaloupe, watermelon, and salad. They unloaded everything and gave it to us.

Two or three of the nearby ranchers came into camp to visit with us. The drought is getting serious. They told us they probably will have to move their cattle out and sell part of them off before the summer is over.

BK June 30-July 3. We left the Cow Creek Reservoir this morning and we're headed for the Camas Reservoir. We have about 15 miles to go today. We got into Camas Reservoir midafternoon. This is a very big reservoir, but it is also really low, there is not much water in it. On the way here, we passed Cathedral Rocks. The big old rocks are piled up and some of them look like skulls. We are going to lay over here at Camas Reservoir for a few days and kind of take it easy. Lots of people camped here for the Fourth of July weekend. Lots of people fishing. Usually this Camas Reservoir is a good fishing spot, but like I say, it's awful low.

BK July 4. We broke camp this morning, left Camas Prairie. We're headed for the Steve Percy Corrals. We got about nine miles to go today so it's going to be a pretty easy day. We got in about 1 o'clock and made camp. We didn't have a special celebration for the Fourth of July. We camped alongside of a creek and have a few trees. This is a pretty good campsite.

Two years ago they had a big fire here in Idaho, and so the trail from here through Syrup Creek and on to Souls Rest has all been closed off. The BLM reseeded that and closed it off and they won't let anybody in there with wagons.

BK July 5. Skinner and I saddled our horses this morning and the BLM will let us go on horseback through the area that burned. We're going to complete the rest of the trail from here to Souls Rest on horseback. We're gonna go up through Syrup Creek. The girls from England and the gal from Portland are going to walk the trail and complete it. We went through and then doubled back. Skinner and I done about 35 miles today. As we were getting back into camp, Skinner looked over at me and he said, "You know what, I don't want to do this ride this far everyday, but you know, you're pretty tough for a guy your age."

I done the trail last year from Independence, Missouri, to Independence, Oregon, and I think this area of the trail out through Syrup Creek was rougher than any part of the trail that I ever saw. It was really steep and it was kind of amazing and makes you wonder how they ever made it through there. There's a place up there on the Syrup Creek Pass—it's about the only place in that whole country that the wagons could have possibly gone through—and I'm sure they did a lot of roughlocking on their wagons, it was really steep.

The Goodale Cutoff that we just went over was also known as the Northern Route of the Oregon Trail. When they were having all the Indian problems at Massacre Rock is when they were using the Goodale Cutoff and this Tim Goodale, his wife was an Indian woman, and at one time he brought a wagon train through on the Goodale Cutoff. They had 300 wagons.

BK July 6. We're back with the wagons and going to Danskine Landing on the North Fork of the Boise River. We had about seven miles of real steep grade going into the Boise River. Danskine Landing is right on the Boise River, it is a pretty country. This is a pretty river. We are camped right on the river. Have a nice camp. On the opposite side of the river is an Indian burial site. There are two big caves. One has a spring in it and a lot of Indian writings on the rocks and I guess at times the Indians camped in these caves, holed up in them.

BK July 7. We broke camp this morning and we're headed for Prairie, Idaho. We got about 12 miles to go today. We've got to pull out of the river, so we got a long grade to pull this morning. It's going to be a long hill. When we got to the top of the long pull, a Basque rancher picked up a couple of the gals and gave them a ride to the ranch. He told them about his holdings. He said he didn't know how much land he had, or how many cattle he had. He said his kids and grandkids all worked on the ranch. Several years before he'd been gathering cows in the mountains and his horse fell and pinned him down. He had to have his leg cut off. We got into Prairie about 3 o'clock. Prairie's a little old, kind of a little old logging town. Not many people live here. It's hay country. Raise a lot of hay around here.

BK July 8. We broke camp and headed for Davidson. We have about 17 miles to do today. This is real steep country, lot of steep pulls today. We're in a lot of timber in this area. We got into camp early afternoon. This is a big meadow and there's an old set of cattle corrals where they used to turn stock out on the

Forest Service allotments. They're not in too good of shape, pretty well run down, but we had a good campsite. Good water, lots of shade.

BK July 9. We left camp and are headed for the little town of Pine, about 17 miles to go today. Pretty steep country, rough country. We got into Pine about 4 o'clock and made camp. We're camped back on the Boise River again. We have a good campsite here. This was our last camp. A lot of the people loaded up and left this evening. Les loaded the mules and went back to the ranch. Skinner and George and myself started sorting things out and breaking down camp. We took the covers off the wagons and got them ready to go home. This is the end of the trail. Wish we could have kept agoing. But came to a stopping point.

BK July 10. Les came back with a big trailer. We loaded all the wagons. Skinner and I and George and Les went back to the ranch. When we got there, we stored everything and put the wagons in the shed under cover.

BK July 11. I went to the corrals and had a talk with the mules and turned them out to pasture. When you spend a lot of time with livestock you get attached to them. I left Les Broadie's today and headed to Oregon to visit my folks.

# End Notes

GENERALLY MOST OF the information in this book is from our personal experiences traveling along the Oregon Trail. We've also relied on personal interviews with Earl Leggett of Aurora, Oregon, conducted by Candy Moulton. For most sections we used *Historic Sites along the Oregon Trail* by Aubrey Haines, *The Oregon Trail Revisited* by Gregory Franzwa, *Women's Voices from the Oregon Trail* by Susan Butruille, and *Women's Diaries of the Westward Journey* by Lillian Schlissel. References from Edwin Bird, William Riley Franklin, Alvin Zaring and Hamilton Scott are from typescript manuscripts located at the Wyoming State Museum. Many other references to historic travelers are from a collection of documents prepared by the U. S. Department of the Interior, National Park Service, as part of a comprehensive management and use plan for the Oregon National Historic Trail. In addition, other information for this book came from the following sources.

**Part One** We used Oregon Trail records at the Wyoming State Museum and American Heritage Center/University of Wyoming. Information about the Aurora, Oregon, wagon, the history of the Aurora Colony and Dr. William Keil is from interviews with Earl Leggett, conducted by Candy Moulton. Some detail also comes from *Roadside History of Oregon* by Bill Gulick.

**Part Two** Detail about Fort Kearny comes from "Fort Kearny" by Myrtle D. Berry, Nebraska State Historical Society, Educational Leaflet No. 7. For this section we also used *The Great Platte River Road* by Merrill Mattes.

**Part Three** For detail about the Texas cattle migrations of the 1870s and 1880s we used articles including, "A Log of the Montana Trail" as kept by Ealy Moore, edited by J. Evetts Haley; "The Texas Trail" by James C. Shaw; "The Proposed National Cattle Trail" by R. D. Holt, "Up the Texas Trail" by John K. Standish; and *American Cattle Trails, 1540–1900* by Garnet M. and Herbert O. Brayer. All of the above materials are located in the Wyoming Stock Growers Association Collection No. 14 at the American Heritage Center/University of Wyoming. We also used *The Great Platte River Road*, cited earlier.

**Part Four** Books used for research in this section included *The Mormon Trek West* by Joseph E. Brown, *Red Cloud and the Sioux Problem*, by

James C. Olson, and *Deer Creek: Frontier Crossing in Pre-territorial Wyoming* by Bill Bryans. We also used manuscript files at the Wyoming State Museum in connection with research conducted by Candy Moulton for *Roadside History of Wyoming.*

**Part Five** Our primary references for this section were *The Mormon Trek West,* cited earlier, and manuscript files at the Wyoming State Museum in connection with research conducted by Candy Moulton for *Roadside History of Wyoming.* We also used *Casper Star-Tribune* newspaper articles published during the summer of 1993, including the excerpts written by Christina Holbrook, Claudette Ortiz, and Deirdre Stoelzle. Much of the information relating to the handcart ordeal of the Mormon pioneers in the Willie and Martin Companies of 1856 is from research conducted by Candy Moulton for *Legacy of the Tetons.* Particularly helpful in writing this section were articles written for the *Casper Star-Tribune* by Joe Marshall. They include Indian oral tribal history and give a very clear picture of the Native Americans' thoughts about the Oregon Trail migration in both historic and modern times. Detail about the 1993 crossing of the Green River is from interviews conducted with wagon train participants October 20–22, 1993, by Candy Moulton. They were originally published in the *Casper Star-Tribune.* For detail about Fort Bridger we used *Experiences of a Forty-Nine*r by William G. Johnston, and *A Brief History of Fort Bridger* by R. S. Ellison. Other sources for this section include *Adventures of Captain Bonneville* by Washington Irving, and *Handcarts to Zion* by Leroy and Ann Hafen.

**Part Six** For this section we found useful *Saddles and Spurs, the Pony Express Saga* by Mary and Raymond Settle and *The Story of the Pony Express* by Glen Danford Bradley.

**Part Seven** We used interviews with Earl Leggett and major sources previously cited.

**Part Eight** Our sources for this final section included *Roadside History of Oregon* by Bill Gulick, major sources previously cited, and interviews with Earl Leggett conducted by Candy Moulton.

**Appendix A** This section about the Goodale Cutoff includes some information from Haines and the Department of Interior documents, but most comes from a journal kept by Ben Kern from June 1 to July 14, 1994. Some detail is from "A little piece of heaven" by Ann Braley in *INEL News* July 5, 1994 and "Modern Pioneers brave Goodale Cutoff" by Linda Phillips in *Intermountain Horse and Rider*, June 24, 1994.

# Bibliography


**BOOK, MAGAZINES AND NEWSPAPERS**

Berry, Myrtle D. "Fort Kearny," Educational Leaflet No. 7. Lincoln: Nebraska State Historical Society, no date.

Bradley, Glenn Danford. *The Story of the Pony Express.* San Francisco: Hesperia House, 1960.

Braley, Anne. "A little piece of heaven," *INEL News*, July 5, 1994.

Brayer, Garnet M. and Herbert O. "American National Cattle Trails, 1540–1900." Western Range Cattle Industry Study and American Pioneer Trails Association, 1952.

Brown, Joseph E. *The Mormon Trek West.* Garden City, NY: Doubleday & Co., 1980.

Bryans, Bill. *Deer Creek: Frontiers Crossroad in Pre-Territorial Wyoming.* Glenrock: Glenrock Historical Commission, 1990.

Butruille, Susan G. *Women's Voices from the Oregon Trail.* Boise: Tamarack Books, 1993.

Ellison, R.S. *Fort Bridger A Brief History.* Cheyenne: Wyoming State Archives, Museums and Historical Department, 1981.

Franzwa, Gregory. *The Oregon Trail Revisited.* St. Louis: The Patrice Press, 1972.

Gardner A. Dudley, William R. Snell and David E. Johnson. "Historic Investigations of the Bear River Divide Segment of the Oregon Trail." Rock Springs, WY: Bureau of Land Management, Wyoming Cultural Resource Series No. 5, 1987

Gulick, Bill. *Roadside History of Oregon.* Missoula: Mountain Press, 1991.

Hafen, Leroy and Ann. *Handcarts to Zion: The Story of a Unique Western Migration, 1856–1860.* Glendale, CA: Arthur H. Clark Company, 1960.

Haines, Aubrey L. *Historic Sites Along the Oregon Trail.* St. Louis: The Patrice Press, 1981.

Hall, Charles "Pat." *Documents of Wyoming Heritage.* Cheyenne: Wyoming Bicentennial Commission, 1976.

Holt, R. D. "The Proposed National Cattle Trail," *Cattleman*, 1943.

Irving, Washington. *The Adventures of Captain Bonneville.* New York: The Co-Operative Publication Society, Inc., no date.

Jording, Mike. *A Few Interested Residents, Wyoming Historical Markers & Monuments.* Helena, MT: Falcon Press, 1992.

Johnston, William G. *Experiences of a Forty-Niner.* Pittsburgh: 1892.

Luchetti, Cathy and Carol Olwell. *Women of the West.* New York: Orion Books, 1982.

Marshall, Joe. "No celebrating Oregon Trail: The other perspective," *Casper Star-Tribune,* "Wyoming Weekend," July 4, 1993.

—. "Tribal 'Holy Road' becomes Oregon Trail," *Casper Star-Tribune,* July 24, 1993.

Mattes, Merrill J. *The Great Platte River Road.* Lincoln: Nebraska University of Nebraska, Bison Books, 1987.

Moore, Ealy, "A Log of the Montana Trail," as edited by J. Evetts Haley, publication data not available.

Moulton, Candy. *Roadside History of Wyoming.* Missoula: Mountain Press Publishing, 1995.

—. "The Oregon Trail," a 10-part series in the *Casper Star-Tribune,* May 2–June 26, 1993.

—. "The Oregon Trail," a collection of 46 news items in the *Casper Star-Tribune,* May-October, 1993.

—. *Legacy of the Tetons.* Boise: Tamarack Books, 1994.

Olson, James. C. *Red Cloud and the Sioux Problem.* Lincoln: University of Nebraska, 1965.

Ortiz, Claudette. "Heading out through Emigrant Gap," *Casper Star-Tribune,* July 14, 1993.

Phillips, Linda. "Modern Pioneers brave Goodale Cutoff," *Intermountain Horse and Rider,* June 24, 1994.

Schlissel, Lillian. *Women's Diaries of the Westward Journey.* New York: Schocken Books, 1982.

Settle, Raymond and Mary. *Saddles and Spurs, the Pony Express Saga.* Harrison, PA: Stackpole Co., 1955.

Shaw, James C. "The Texas Trail" publication data not given.

Standish, John K. "Up the Texas Trail," *The Producer, the National Livestock Monthly,* 1932.

Stoelzle, Deirdre. "Falling in love cure for trail blues," *Casper Star-Tribune,* July 9, 1993.

United States Department of the Interior, National Park Service. *Comprehensive Management and Use Plan, Oregon National Historic Trail,* Appendix II, August 1981.

United States Department of the Interior, National Park Service. *Comprehensive Management and Use Plan, Oregon National Historic Trail,* Appendix III, August 1981.

United States Department of the Interior, National Park Service, *Comprehensive Management and Use Plan, Oregon National Historic Trail,* Appendix D, no date.

**INTERVIEWS**

Personal and telephone interviews were conducted by Candy Moulton with Ben Kern, Phil Marincic, and Earl Leggett between May 1993 and December 1994.

**OVERLAND TRAIL DIARIES, JOURNALS, AND OTHER WRITINGS**

Bailey, Marilla R. (Huntington Library).

Bird, Edwin, Wyoming State Museum, typescript copy; (original in Ayer Collection, Newberry Library, Chicago).

Breyfogle, Joshua. *Historic Sites Along the Oregon Trail*; (Overland Journal, ms.; Original in Dartmouth College Collection, Hanover, N.H.)

Bridger, Jim. Wyoming State Museum, file located at Fort Bridger State Historic Site.

Bruff, J. Goldsborough. *Gold Rush: [His] Journals, Drawings, and Other Papers*, ed. Georgia Willis Read and Ruth Gaines. New York: 1944.

Bryant, Edwin. *What I Saw in California*. New York: 1849. (National Park Service).

Buckingham, Harriet Talcott. *Women's Voices From the Oregon Trail.* (Diary. Oregon Historical Society, Portland, OR.)

Burnett, Peter H. "Recollections & Opinions of an Old Pioneer." *Oregon Historical Quarterly*, 5. March 1904. (Ayer Collection, Newberry Library, Chicago).

Burton, Sir Richard F. *The City of Saints*. New York: Harper & Brothers Publishers,1862.

Carpenter, Helen. *Women's Voices From the Oregon Trail.* "A Trip Across the Plains."

Chislett, John. "The 1856 Handcart Disaster." Rock Springs, WY: U.S. Bureau of Land Management.

Clayton, William. "Journal, A Daily Record..." Salt Lake City: 1921.

Collins, Caspar. Letter to his mother, June 16, 1862, typescript copy Wyoming State Museum.

Cross, Osborne. "Historic Sites Along the Oregon Trail" from Journal, in Settle [ed.] *March of the Mounted Riflemen.* Glendale: 1940.

Cummins, Sarah. *Autobiography and Reminiscences.* La Grande, Oregon: 1914.

De Smet, Father Pierre J. *Life, Letters and Travels,* ed. H. M. Chittenden. 4 vols. Cleveland: 1905.

Duniway, Abigail Scott. *Captain Gray's Company,* Portland: 1859.

Eels, Myra. "Diary, April–September, 1838," in Drury [ed.] *First White Women Over the Rockies,* 71–89. Glendale: 1963.

Field, Matthew C. *Prairie and Mountain Sketches,* ed. Kate L. Gregg. Norman: 1957.

Franklin, William Riley. Wyoming State Museum, typescript manuscript.

Geer, Elizabeth. "Diary...," *Transactions,* Oregon Pioneer Association: 1907. (Oregon Historical Society).

Hastings, Loren B. "Diary of...a Pioneer...," *Transactions,* Oregon Pioneer Association: 1923. (Oregon Historical Society).

Hill, John B. "Gold" *Annals of Wyoming,* No. 9, April 1933-January 1935.

Lienhard, Heinrich. *From St. Louis to Sutter's Fort,* ed. E.G. and E. K. Gudde. Norman: University of Oklahoma,1961.

Nesmith, James W. "Diary of the Emigration," *Oregon Historical Quarterly,* VII: December 1906.

Parker, Rev. Samuel. *Journal of an Exploring Tour Beyond the Rocky Mountains.* Ithica, NY: 1944.

Parkman, Francis. *The Oregon Trail.* (Harrisburg, PA: The National Historical Society, 1993).

Pratt, Orson. *Latter-Day Saints Millenial Star,* XI, (1849); XII (1850).

Price, Joseph. "The Road to California: Letters of Joseph Price" ed. Thomas Marshall, *Mississippi Valley Historical Review,* IX September, 1924.

Pringle, Virgil. "Diary...," *Transactions,* Oregon Pioneer Association 1920. (Oregon Historical Society).

Pritchard, James A. *Historic Sites Along the Oregon Trail from the Overland Diary of James A. Pritchard, Kentucky to California,* ed. Dale L. Morgan. Denver: 1959.

Rudd, Lydia. *Women's Diaries of the Westward Journey.* "Notes by the Wayside En Route to Oregon, 1852."

Scott, Hamilton. Wyoming State Museum, journal, typescript, with notes by Alvin Zaring.

Stansbury, Capt. Howard. *Exploration and Survey of the Valley of the Great Salt Lake...* Washington, D. C.: 1853.

Stewart, Helen. *Women's Voices From The Oregon Trail.* ("Diary of Helen Stewart, 1853": Eugene, Oregon: The Lane County Pioneer-Historical Society, 1961).

Talbot, Theodore *Historic Sites Along the Oregon Trail* (Journals, 1843 and 1849–52, ed. Charles H. Carey. Portland: 1931)

Townsend, John K. *Narrative of a Journey Across the Rocky Mountains... Early Western Travels*, ed. R. G. Thwaites. Cleveland: 1905.

Wakeman, Bryarly, and Vincent Geiger. *Trail to California*, ed. David M. Potter. New Haven: 1945.

Warner, Elizabeth Stewart. *Women's Voices From the Oregon Trail* (Letter 1856 or 1857, published with Diary, 1853, Agnes Stewart. Eugene, Oregon: Lane County Historical Society, 1959).

Williams, Lucia Lorain. *Women's Voices From the Oregon Trail.* (Letter to her mother, September 16, 1851. Mrs. Helen Stratton Felker.)

# *Index*

*The text is composed in*
*twelve-point Adobe Garamond.*
*The display face is Adobe Ex Ponto.*
*Secondary display is Lutahline*
*by Judith Sutcliffe: the Electronic Typographer.*
*The book is printed on*
*sixty-pound Gladtfelter Supple Opaque,*
*an acid-free, recyled text stock.*

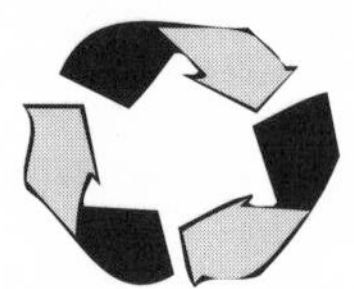

# Wagon Wheels

OTHER BOOKS BY CANDY MOULTON:

*Steamboat: Legendary Bucking Horse*
*Legacy of the Tetons*
*Roadside History of Wyoming*

# Wagon Wheels

## A Contemporary Journey on the Oregon Trail

*with a foreword by*
*Kathleen O'Neal Gear*

Candy Moulton
& Ben Kern

HIGH PLAINS PRESS

Manufactured in the United States of America.

FIRST PRINTING

9 8 7 6 5 4 3 2 1

*Cover art on the softcover edition is by BJ Durr.*

**Library of Congress Cataloging-in-Publication Data**

Moulton, Candy Vyvey, 1955-
Wagon wheels : a contemporary journey on the Oregon Trail / Candy Moulton & Ben Kern ; with a foreword by Kathleen O'Neal Gear.
p. cm.
Includes bibliographical references and index.
ISBN 0-931271-36-3 (soft : alk. paper)
ISBN 0-931271-37-1 (hardcover : alk. paper)
1. Oregon Trail--Description and travel.
2. Wagons--Oregon Trail.
3. Frontier and pioneer life--Oregon Trail.
I. Kern, Ben.
II. Title.
F597.M77 1996 96-17581
917.804'2--dc20 CIP

HIGH PLAINS PRESS
539 CASSA ROAD
GLENDO, WYOMING 82213